# SUPERHERO

## DISCOVERING THE MAN THAT SLEEPS WITHIN

### KEITH LYVELL BROOKS

To: KEVIN JR,

God HAS A PLAN FOR YOUR LIFE
THAT ONLY you CAN ACCOMPLISH!

you ARE A SUCCESS!
you ARE A SUPERHERO!!!

4.3.10

# The True Superhero

A Superhero is not just some cartoon character.

A Superhero is a man that's committed to demonstrating the character of his creator. – "God"

A Superhero retaliates with love against his enemy even when his enemy has done wrong against him. He never ever keeps record of a suffered wrong.

He forgives the unforgivable, makes peace with the unpeaceable.

He laughs at pain and anything that tries to destroy him. Why? Because he knows that's what strengthens him.

A Superhero has the ability to respond to any and all things. When slackness or slothfulness tries to creep on him it has to bow down in his presence because of the King in him.

When a Superhero opens his mouth his words shoots out like arrows destined to hit its target. The bull's-eye of success is his results in life.

A Superhero does not have to demand respect, respect demands him!

A Superhero does not have to defend himself, righteous defense defends him.

A Superhero winks his eye at fear! Knowing that the power of love generates his faith.

If a Superhero falls he quickly rises back to the top because he understands the love of his father "God".

He is secure in himself; he knows where his true identity lies within.

A Superhero is bold, smart, confident, diligent, consistent, and persistent. He does what others are afraid to step out and do! This is why his name will be remembered.

A woman's words of encouragement brings him satisfaction, but accomplishments of purpose brings him fulfillment.

Victory is in his blood and he often reflects on the star in the east that shined on his savior when he was an infant. Reminding him that a Superhero was born to save the day.

# Dedication

This book is dedicated to my spiritual father.
I could never find the words to express my thanks for helping me become the man that I am today.

Trials and tribulations have come my way because of bad choices. When others look down on me, you continue smiling, knowing I'll prevail someday. Like God, you know my heart.

Dr. Creflo A. Dollar, Jr., it's an honor to say that you are indeed my superhero.

Your encouraging words have been the key to my success.

**As a man thinketh in his heart, so is he.**
**Proverbs 23:7**

# Special Thanks

I'd also like to thank those who helped facilitate my incarceration. While your contribution was painful, it was worth it.

Why?

If it hadn't been for you, and my disobedient decision of breaking the law.
I probably would never had the opportunity to write this book to empower the hearts of men.

# TABLE OF CONTENTS

# BROOKS, KEITH LYVELL

GDC ID: 0001150320

| PHYSICAL DESCRIPTION | | | |
|---|---|---|---|
| **YOB:** 1973 | **RACE:** BLACK | | **GENDER:** MALE |
| **HEIGHT:** 6'01" | **WEIGHT:** 200 | **EYE COLOR:** BROWN | **HAIR COLOR:** BLACK |

Dear Hero,

This is the month of March of 2005. I'm now sitting on my bunk; the top bunk of beds, bunk 56 that is. I now only have a pen that's about to run out of ink, and a used note book pad that one of the inmates gave me. Pens, papers, and honey buns are like gold, silver and diamonds in prisons, especially when there's no money on your books. Even though this pen can die out at anytime and with only 10 pieces of paper, I'm going to just start writing my very own first book. I don't know right now how I'm going to get a new pen or even 10 more sheets of paper, but I'm going to finish what I've started. Can you believe it! I got a whole book on the inside of me waiting to appear on the outside. I wasn't so good in English class I think I passed with a D. So I really don't understand punctuations and things like that! Na! I ain't gone quit! If I quit then you will die not so much as physically but spiritually. Why? Because I have so much to give, give what? You may ask. To give you the knowledge of discovering who you really are. O.K. Here I go, I trust god man! I've got until Sept 8, 2005 to finish. I believe I can do it. I have time, I'm committed, I'm getting nervous, my hands are sweating, there's no privacy, and it's loud in here. What do I expect I'm locked in a cage with 79 other men; a fight just broke out in back of me. No need to see who it is, I gotta stay focus! I gotta get started, I'm out.


BROOKS

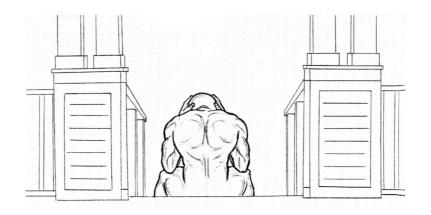

# Chapter One

## Super Section One: A place called "nowhere"

*The eyes of the Lord are in every place, keeping watch upon the evil and the good.(Proverbs 15:3)*

### "Ronnie"

Look here, man, I'm about to expose myself. Can I trust you? Can I trust that you won't tell anyone about what's going on in my raggedy life? I know that asking you if I can trust you sounds crazy. But I need to talk to someone. I need someone who'll really listen. I need someone who won't start laughing at me!

My wife did that to me every time I tried to open and share my heart. When I started my lawn care business, things were going well. Therefore, she was doing well. My wife had everything any woman could ever need or want. She was happy. Seeing her happy filled me with joy. However, she was bossy as well as happy. My wife was always a take-charge type of woman. Instead of putting my foot down at times, I let her have her way! I didn't want any trouble. So, I kept my mouth closed and let her run everything. Now, I've got thousands of dollars worth of trouble. My wife's weekly shopping sprees during our two years together left me with $36,000 in credit card debt. By the way, she became my ex-wife about two months ago. Why? She said our money problems were making her feel insecure! I cut off my right hand while working on my riding lawnmower blade. Can you believe that! She left me because I couldn't maintain the lifestyle to which she'd become accustomed. Whatever happened to "for better or for worse"? She said I was weak! That reminds me of what my family and friends would say about me. I was always being run over!

Now my business is about to crumble. I don't know which way to turn. Which way would you turn? Do you know? I feel like no one cares. I'm about to lose it! I really came close the day I saw my ex-wife at a red light when I pulled up in my rusted-out green Ford pickup. She was sitting in a silver drop-top Mercedes-Benz, with rims that outshone the sun itself. She was holding hands with and kissing another man. Balloons–tied to the rearview mirror–bobbed in the air. As the light turned green, the Benz pulled away. My ex turned and looked back at me, shaking her head as if to say, "Now that's a shame."

This hurts, man! I feel abandoned! Most of this was my fault. I should have stood up for myself. I was too passive. Where did I get that? Why am I so weak? Maybe you think I'm weak as well. What about you– are you weak? Do you let circumstances and other people control you? Are you about to lose it? Come on, I'm being honest with you. Can you be honest with me? I don't have a sense of belonging! No one wants my services or me. I've never felt accepted. Maybe you don't accept me either.

One day, while getting some gas at the gas station, a young man gave me a fluorescent green flyer that said, _Try Jesus._ I said to myself, "Yeah, right! What can Jesus do for me? No one else has accepted me, so why would I think that he will?"

Everyone else has abandoned me. I'm all alone. I feel...I feel I'm at a place in my life called "nowhere."

## "Diaz"

What's up, Homie? Yeah, I'm back from the big house. I'm stepping off a Greyhound bus with my beige Dickies, a white button-up shirt, a pair of black Chuck Taylors, and my blue jacket: The newly-released prisoner's official uniform.

What's so funny, amigo? I'm talking to you. Oh, I see. I'm just a convict to you, right? You assume I'm a threat to society, don't you? I'm taking time out and writing to you. I want to share how I feel. But, no, you laugh. You see me in a prison outfit and think what others think: "Diaz, the ex-convict." My family has always laughed at me. I could never do anything right. No one ever believed in me, including my own mother! My homies believed in me more than my entire family.

They showed me the most love. At least, that's what I thought when I started hanging out with them. However, when the police raided the place where we sold drugs, they all snitched on me to the ghetto police! As we waited for our sentence, I sat there in a cold sweat. I hoped and prayed God would get me out of this one! My grandmother said God could save anyone. He didn't spare me that day. I got a mandatory seven years in the State Penitentiary. My homies only got one year of probation. They went back to their cells to exchange those big, orange clown suits for street clothes and were released. They laughed as they passed me in the courtroom.

What's wrong with me? How come people call me stupid and laugh at me? Why can't I do anything right? Look at me, amigo! Seven years of my life have gone down the drain. Since I'm writing to you, let me ask you something. Yeah, amigo, I'm still talking to you. Are you one of those Christians like my grandmother was? The reason I ask is because I want to know why the God you serve kills people? Why does He cause car wrecks and plane crashes if you mess up and sin? Why does God severely punish a bunch of people, like the residents of New Orleans?

Why didn't God help me get out of trouble? I mean, I prayed. But prayer didn't work for me! Why, amigo, why? Oh, I know–because God doesn't like me either! I know He's in heaven laughing at me also, amigo!

There ain't no use putting applications in for work. They are going to tell me what they tell every convict: "I'm sorry, sir, but we cannot hire you because you have a felony on your record." Okay, I did my time for the crime, but please don't stop me from getting mine. I want to do right. I want to work. Things seem hopeless because society won't give me a second chance! But I see what's going on, amigo, they're setting me up to fail again. If they let my past keep me from getting work, they know I could go back to my old ways. I don't feel good about myself. Who am I? Why can't I be a normal guy with a home, car, family and a good-paying job? That's the American dream that I'll never see come true. I mean, what woman wants to be with an ex-convict? Who's going to trust me? Would you trust me?

I got nowhere to go and no one to turn to. You...you're the only person in whom I can confide. It's you, amigo. I'm a lost man. Amigo, you wouldn't snitch on me, right? If things don't get better, I'll be back on the streets again trying to make a fast buck or two.

I tried that Jesus stuff. But He let me down. He wasn't there for me in that courtroom. Where was God then, amigo? Where is He now?

A little, shriveled-up old man on 45th Street says he's a Christian. He sells newspapers for a living. He's always telling me I don't know who I am in Christ. I just blow him off. I don't even understand what he means. I'm kind of fed up with this Christian stuff! I met some in prison, but they weren't so heavenly! They're some of the worst people you'd ever want to meet! Amigo, I knew the prison choir director, who led the prison choir during the Sunday morning chapel service. He was a good choir director, but music wasn't his only talent. He pleasured every prisoner he could with homosexual activity! So you tell me, amigo, what good is being a Christian if they do what the world does?

I feel dead. I have no hope, no energy and no more dreams. I'm hungry. I don't think I can take this much longer, amigo! There's no more meaning to my life. Do your prayers work amigo? If so, pray for me! I gotta do what I gotta do! I don't know if you understand what I'm feeling. I feel...I feel...come on, amigo! Don't look down on me or laugh at me. I feel like I'm at a place called "nowhere."

## "Roscoe"

During the summer, it's extremely hot down here in Texas. Not only am I physically hot, but I'm hot with myself! You know, within, I just hate myself! I'm confused, miserable, agitated with my life and life itself. I oversee 437 employees as a tractor-trailer supervisor at one of the nation's largest trucking companies. But I still don't have any peace within myself! I'm writing to you to see if you can understand me, because no one seems to understand the real me. That includes the little preacher down yonder. He just told me to pray about it. I've prayed and prayed. Things have just gotten worse!

Hey, listen! Don't you go running off at the mouth at what I'm about to tell you, cowboy! I'm talking to you. Man, last night I beat my wife in front of the kids. Ah, come on, cowboy, you're not one of those perfect Christians, are you? Why did I beat my wife? She pissed me off! What did she do? She really didn't do anything. She forgot to wash my last set of underwear. Plus, the bills are due and I'm behind! My dad beat mama, whenever he got mad. I hated watching and hearing that! When I do it, I picture my dad punching and kicking my mama. So, I'm doing exactly what I hated, when things don't go right! Yeah, I'm abusive. I know. It hurts to be this way. I bully my family and my employees. I appear to be very vicious and strong on the outside. But on the inside, I'm a weak man.

I'm a tough cowboy and know the trucking game better than the best of them. But there's a little boy on the inside that should grow up but doesn't know how! I'm lost, cowboy. What do you think I should do?

Church! I don't have time for church! My wife threatened to divorce me last night. What am I going to do if she and the kids leave? I'm a nobody and I feel very empty inside. My back is surely against the wall now and it won't be long that until I'll be lying in a casket! I'm really thinking about driving one of those semi rigs up to Tennessee and rolling it off of one of those big mountains. I don't want to hurt any more. Now, that's an answer for hurt and pain. Don't you agree?

If God put me here on the earth, why did he do it? Just so I can hurt?! Who am I? Where do I belong? Why can't people accept me? I have so many questions and need answers. Where do I go from here, cowboy? So much pressure! How much more can a man bear? I'm writing this letter at a truck stop. Hold on, my cell phone is ringing. Give me a second, cowboy. Okay, I'm back. That was my 19-year-old daughter. She said the police have a warrant for my arrest. I asked her, "For what?" My wife pressed charges against me for what happened last night. They charged me with aggravated assault because I threw an ashtray and it busted her head! Cowboy, I told you I live a miserable life.

Listen, cowboy, thanks for reading this letter. It was nice talking to you. I'm heading on up to Tennessee to end this. I feel...(crying) I feel...that I'm at a place called "nowhere."

### "Light"

What's up, brother? They call me Light. Why? I'm quick as light! Just like when you turn on your light switch and light appears– that's how extremely quick I am on the football field. I play football for one of the worst teams of the league. We're getting ready to play one of the biggest games of the year.

I am a defensive end who stands at 6'6" and weighs 245 pounds.

But I can run a 40-yard dash in less than 5 seconds! My job is to knock the day lights out of the quarterback before he passes the ball and makes a completion for a first down or touchdown.

That's not my only job. There's nothing like being paid big money for what you love to do. Keep this in mind: Your gift or talent will always put you on the path to success. My other "job" is being a drug addict. Yeah, I said drug addict! I'm addicted to crack and meth. Please listen to me. It's one thing to have 90,000 people booing you over a missed tackle. But it's totally different when you get booed by one person who really knows your weakness, who ostracizes you and spreads your business all over the world. I'm sitting in an empty locker room, writing this letter to you before my teammates arrive.

Man, I have money and a fast car. Women, just like cocaine, are everywhere. You can get and use them any time of the day. I'm the best at my position in the league. I'm the most valuable player of the league. Yes, I can have any woman. Yes, I have a personal yacht. Yes, I have four homes: one on the West coast, another on the East Coast, one at the North Pole and the last at the South Pole. Florida is lovely, I must say. But none of that compares to the loneliness I feel.

I need help, man! Can you help me? People think I don't need any help. I've successfully put up quite a front. However, Light's light is getting dimmer by the second. Football is what I do. A crack addict is who I am. It's true, man and it hurts! I can't stop, man! I've got to hurry and finish writing. I'm jonesing for my pre-game hit! Yeah, I play high all the time. I don't need a can of some sports energy drink. You just give me my crack and I'm good to go.

Then when the high is gone, I'm back to square one. I'm lonely and full of regret! My head hurts at times and I always feel weak. I really don't know what to do.

Now, I've got something I must tell you. If I didn't tell you I'd feel like I'm not keeping it real with you. But, please, man, don't repeat what I'm about to tell you. If you blow it, the whole team and the coaching staff will know, not to mention the media. Keep your mouth shut, okay?!

I've got HIV. I don't know which woman got me, but she's out there. I guess my uncle was right, when sin is fully matured it will bring death. Hey man, it's me, Light, the famous football player. I'm going to die from an incurable disease. What did you just say? I'm talking to you, the one reading this letter. What do you mean that Jesus can heal me? Don't you know all the wrong I've done? It would be stupid for me to ask God for help. He's mad at me. He doesn't like me either!

There's no answer, do you agree? What about your life? What negative job are you working on? Are you perfect? If so, can you show me how to become perfect? Is that possible?

I'm sitting alone in a locker room. At this point in my life, I have the best and the worst. I don't know if that makes sense to you. I'll give you an example. The HIV virus is one of the most vicious diseases around.

If HIV could speak, it would say it's the MVP of all diseases. I have it all and am about to lose it all. I feel...I feel like I'm at a place called "nowhere."

The aforementioned four men have found themselves in a place called "nowhere." Rich and poor men have been broken and forsaken. Money doesn't really matter when you have got nowhere to go. However, it could prove useful if he had "a purpose that's going somewhere."

A man with power who abuses his authority by shaming and hurting others is a man without character. A man with no character will always be in a place called "nowhere."

Were you able to see yourself in any of those men? I know I could. It was awful to feel that way. Now, I'm not speaking of a physical place, but a spiritual place. For example, you take an ambitious artist who expects to win an art competition, but learns he lost. After hearing that news, he goes to a park and sits on a bench with his face in his hands, with a torn heart and a broken spirit.

He doesn't know if he should give up. This is the point where men destroy the future God has prepared for them. Quitters never experience victory. Victorious men never quit. If you're a man who's quit or is pondering about quitting, just know that sometime in your life, your spirit has been wounded.

If you feel this way right now, you're not alone. Great men of God in the Bible have felt the same way. King David had a broken spirit. Even great men of God today, the ones you may know personally or have seen on TV or read about, have experienced that feeling. But they rose above that cloud and entered the limitless skies of sunshine. They headed to a place called "somewhere," a place that's life-fulfilling.

You see, man of God, when a man doesn't know Christ Jesus, he'll always be stuck "nowhere." But a man who's determined to find out who he is in Christ, what's been created for him, and uses what's he's learned about himself—he will become his own superhero. Could I be talking about you? It can be! This book aims to help you discover the real you. You should be fed up with the average life you have been living. Your heavenly father wants to give you more. He wants you to discover all the powers he's invested in you. This book isn't for everyone. If you have already discovered who you are in Christ, I urge you to pass this book along to a man who hasn't yet made that discovery.

I remember being locked away in prison. It was so dark. The atmosphere was so negative. However, I found light in the midst of it all. The light began shining when God began speaking to me. I heard Him say, "Keith, here and now you have the time to really find out and develop who you truly are in my son, Christ."

I decided to dive into the word of God and really find out who I am! What I discovered was funny to me. After being a member at World

Changers Church International for six years and spending a year with my spiritual father, Creflo Dollar, the seeds of self-knowledge began springing upon a daily basis as I meditated on God's word.

Then I began to see hundreds of men around me who didn't have a clue who they were. They were good men who'd made bad choices. They didn't know who they were. That was my problem.

I began to open God's word in an environment where men are very angry, hostile, and selfish. I showed them who they really were in Christ. I developed a passion to see the light bulb come on when a man discovers his identity. You don't have to be in prison to be miserable. The four men that you read about at the beginning of this chapter were in a self-made prison. It was prison built on self-ignorance. Yes, that's what I'm saying. When you don't' know who you are in Christ, the anointed one, you are just like an inmate in a prison which is actually the palm of the Enemy's hand.

While in prison, I thought about you and believed God moved me to use a gift that was new to me. It's the gift of writing. Therefore, I began to write this book so that you too can discover the superhero that is asleep within you.

This book is backed up by God's word! Take what you read and apply it with everything you got! You'll be a successful man! You'll be a perfect demonstration of a superhero, a man with the character and powers of God. If you're in prison now, it may seem like your life is over. You feel like you're going nowhere, but you can change the words Satan is saying by taking advantage of the time you have left and using this book to discover who you are.

Men who seem free, but are prisoners to the bondage of not knowing who they are in Christ, add balance to your life by taking time out and following your lead to become who they are in Jesus Christ.

A place called "nowhere" is definitely not the place where God created you to be. It could be various places. However, know this: Wherever God chooses for you to be, the superhero in you is needed there.

As you read this book, accept that you no longer exist in a place called "nowhere". Meditate on the truth of going to a place that you have never gone before, a place where you'll win 24/7 all the days of your life. Keep your head up and soar on, superhero, soar on.

# Chapter Two

## Super Section One: "You are just like your daddy!"

"Mario, Mario, come here right now!"

"Yes, ma'am," he responded.

"Why did you punch Kimmy in the eye?" the teacher asked.

"Because she knocked down my stack of Legos and she made me mad!" Mario said.

Kimmy then responded, "I was only trying to help you!"

"I didn't need your help. You are acting just like mama—she was always trying to help Daddy out and he used to tell her he didn't need her help. But she kept on getting in the way and it made him mad and he always punched her out."

"That was your daddy, Mario. You are not him! And that does not give you any right to hit Kimmy in the eye!" the teacher said.

"Well, the reason why I did it was because I saw my daddy do it, and my mama always tells me, 'Mario, you are just like your daddy!'"

"Mario, Mario, turn that Playstation off and get in here right now!" his stepfather shouted from the family room.

"Yes, sir." Mario replied.

"Why did you not do what I asked you to do?"

"I did rake up all the leaves in the yard," Mario answered.

"Well, that wasn't good enough!" his stepfather barked. "And since you didn't do a very good job, you won't be going to the Middle School Dance with your friends! Why can't you be like the other teenage boys around here? They do their chores. They wash and vacuum their vehicles and they even take out the trash! What's wrong with you? You're not so bright, are you?"

"I don't know," Mario said, looking at the ground.

"Well, I know one thing your mother told me all about your daddy! She said he was lazy, up to no good and he made a living by selling drugs! Not only did he sell drugs, he used them and they fried his brain! Maybe that's what's wrong with your brain. No wonder you are so lazy. You can't do anything good! I can see right now you're not going to amount to anything! You'll never ever be successful!"

Mario, head still down, began crying as his stepfather continued, "Everyone in the family and even your friends will make it in life, but you...you are just like your daddy, a dead man walking around."

"Mario! Mario! You son of a gun! What was that? You couldn't even catch a cold if you had to."

Everyone on the practice field all started laughing at Coach Wilson's comments after Mario dropped his tenth pass from the quarterback.

"Give me fifty pushups and two laps around the entire football field. But before that, I'd I like to call a team meeting."

In the middle of the meeting Coach Wilson said, "Gentlemen, I must say that I was pleased with this morning's practice. It was very physical and energetic, and you also were focused and enthusiastic! Good job, guys! We can go really far this year."

Before ending the meeting, Coach Wilson said, "Mario, you said when you made the team that your biggest and most fulfilling dream was to play in the NFL. It's okay to dream sometimes, but that's one dream you'll never accomplish. How do you expect to play professional football when you can't even catch?"

The whole team started laughing as Coach Wilson continued, "You'll never ever make it in the NFL, not with those butter fingers! You're slow, clumsy and not too smart. The only reason you made this football team was because you came to practice every day and were never late. I've been coaching here at this high school for the last thirty years and I remember coaching your daddy. When I first saw him perform in practice, I just knew he wasn't going to make it. He was slow as mud, always missing tackles. He only weighed a buck fifty and his legs were skinnier than an ostrich!"

The team kept laughing while Mario hung his head. This seemed to be the most embarrassing moment in his life. Trying to avoid crying, he looked up and around with a fake smile, wishing that the Coach would shut up and end the meeting.

But Coach Wilson kept on, "I hope I'm not offending you, but I just had to tell you the truth. You'll never make it! You'll never make it! No potential whatsoever! So what are you going to do–quit the football team and drop out of high school, just like your daddy did?"

"No, sir! I plan on being successful in life, graduating from high school and going to college."

"College! Ha, ha, ha," the coach laughed. "Let me tell you something before I let you go do what you owe me for dropping ten passes in a row. I can look in your eyes and tell you one thing: Hell will freeze over before you make it at anything in life. And here's a fact that you better not ever forget–you're just like your sorry daddy."

Guess who walked across the stage June 7 to receive his high school diploma? Mario! That's right! Mario graduated from high school, although he was a little slow in the learning department. With determination and hours of studying, he managed to succeed, but that's not all. Mario earned an art scholarship to one of the America's finest universities. Mario's stepfather was shocked. His mother was surprised, but glad. His whole family was very excited for him. While they were scratching their heads, everyone seemed to look at Mario a little differently now. They no longer saw him as just like his father. Mario was the first in his family to go college. Mario was now doing something positive with his life. Mario had made up in his mind that he *wouldn't* be just like his daddy.

After six months in college, Mario maintained a C average, not so bad and not so good. He didn't have the same determination to do great that he had in high school. One of Mario's problems was surrounding himself with positive friends. However, the positive friends with As and Bs rejected Mario because they knew he was slow. They nicknamed him "just can't get it right." Smart and beautiful women were all around Mario. He tried to get to know them. However, they all rejected him.

"No, I'm sorry. You're the weird guy, everyone talks about. I'm not about to let people call me weird because I hang out with you."

Mario began experiencing the same thing back home. Insecurities, worries, inferiority and rejection began rising like a morning fog. Mario found a different group of friends who experienced the same pains of rejection. However, they were the wrong kind of friends. Now, his grades went from C's to D's because of heavy partying, drug use, alcohol and sex. After just getting by during his sophomore year, he was headed to his junior year.

One day, as Mario was on his way to the art lab, a young woman ran him down from behind.

"Mario, Mario, stop! Please stop! I really need to speak with you."

At first, Mario didn't remember the girl. She said, "Do you remember me? I'm Shannon. I left the concert with you and our friends and went to the party and we all got really drunk. We began to talk, laugh and play wrestle with one another. We went into your dorm and had sex. We woke up the next morning in the same bed. I was going to keep this to myself, but I couldn't. I had, at least, to tell you what's going on. I haven't had sex with anyone but you."

"Come on!" Mario said, "Get to the point!" Now he remembered the girl.

She burst into tears: "I'm pregnant! I'm pregnant, I'm sorry but...but I'm pregnant!"

Mario snapped, "How do you know it's mine?"

She sobbed, "...Because you were the last person I had sex with!"

"I don't believe you! I want a DNA test!"

"Okay Mario, that's fine! I'm sorry."

The DNA test came back positive. Mario was the father. He accepted the fact that he had a baby on the way. So he dropped out of college and found a job in a factory.

Disappointment filled his mother's heart. His stepfather, family and friends were stunned, but just for a moment. They all thought the same thing: It had been too good to be true. Many people would remark, "Your daddy has kids all over the globe. You are going to allow history to repeat itself. You are just like your daddy."

Mario is now 31 years old. He was 19 years old when he dropped out of college. Both you and I can agree that Mario hasn't had a pleasant life. What happened to Mario's life after he dropped out of college? Did things get better or worse? Read on.

"I'm going to call the police!"

"Mama, please don't. I promise you I'll take care of everything."

"Mario, I am tired of this mess! This is the second time there's been a drive-by and my house has been shot up! All because of you and selling them drugs! You need to stop doing this, son. You or someone else can end up dead! There are other ways of getting money–getting it the fast way won't last very long."

The Bible says:

*Wealth gained by dishonesty will be diminished, but he who gathers by labor will increase. (Proverbs 13:11)*

"Son, why don't you slow down and go get you an honest job? Selling drugs won't last. You know what happened to your daddy when they raided his house. Instead of surrendering, he wanted to play cowboys and Indians, and he ended up getting shot in the head and dying right there inside of a drug house! It's a shame that I have to repeat myself! Mario, you have seven kids scattered across the country. What happens when you end up in jail or your grave?"

"I understand what you're saying, Mama, but no one will hire me! I'm making a lot more money than when I worked at the factory. I was fired because they said I couldn't catch on quickly enough! They said I was too slow. Every time I go to a job interview, they give me those I.Q. tests and I always fail. There's no hope for me! Everyone always rejects me! To be honest with you, I wish I could end my life now! I have seven babies' mamas calling constantly, begging for money. Three of them are threatening me, if I don't start paying for child support. There are people out there trying to take me–"Oreo"–out! Not only that, they are after my family, too! Those other drug dealers are jealous of me because I make more money than they do. I can't help it Mama. I...I just can't help it!"

"Excuses, excuses, excuses–just like your daddy. Mario, there's a job somewhere out there for you. Son, I hate to say it, but if you don't change jobs, you'll find yourself in one of two places. One–in a state prison, where you'll be scrubbing toilets! Two–in Hell as Satan's personal fire manager, making sure the fire doesn't burn out!"

"Yeah, right, Mama! Thanks for the encouragement!"

"Any time, son–and yes, you're right. I'm trying to encourage you to stop what you're doing. You can't say that I didn't warn you. I recall saying the same thing before your daddy died. Son, do what he didn't do and listen."

Mario answered his ringing cell phone. "Yo, this is Oreo."

The other voice said, "Do you have the package and the money?"

Mario responded, "Yea, you know it! It's on! Meet me at Joe's Pancake and Waffles across the street from the hotel on 95th Street."

"Cool. Peace out."

Mario hung up the phone.

"Well, I gotta go, Mama, and I'll make sure the drive-by won't happen again."

"Mario, before you go I want to tell you something I told your father before he died," his mama said.

"Okay, what's that, Mama?" Mario asked.

"Always listen to that small voice that says, *No*. I love you, son."

"I love you, too, Mama. I'll see you later."

It's close to 5 p.m. as Mario walks down the steps of his mother's porch. He hears a small voice inside saying, "*No*, Mario. Don't deliver that package. *No*, Mario. Don't go to that restaurant and meet that guy. *No*, Mario. Don't even get in your truck. Go back inside your mother's house now!"

Mario stands in front of his mother's home, eying the bullet holes sprayed across the siding from last night's shooting. He wonders if he should listen to that little voice in his head. He knows nothing about Satan and his evil devices. Satan comes to kill, steal, and destroy and he is powerful. You'll see that, as you read this book. Satan has one particular very effective strategy: the power of suggestion! Does Satan's strategy of suggestion work on Mario? Read on.

After the warning voice, Mario hears another voice, seemingly his own thoughts, "Man, Oreo, you mean to tell me you're going to pass upon that blockbuster deal? This will put you right at $2.2 million. Come on, Oreo, you ain't no punk! Remember–you're Oreo! You're the baddest boy in the game! Make this your last drop. Then you can get out of the game with $2.2 million under your belt! What about your kids? They need food in their mouths; they need clothes on their backs. You know what'll happen if you don't pay them three knucklehead girls. They'll be calling the Child Support Office. Then, you're really going to be broke and working a factory job for free, because they're going to get all your money. Don't be a fool, Oreo. Just this one last drop! Think, Oreo, $2.2 million! It's all about you, Oreo. You got the world on lock down. Ha, ha, ha."

Mario says out loud, "I can do this! I can do this!" as he stands in the middle of the street lifting both arms with his fists clenched together as though he just won a heavyweight title. His mother looks out the window and shakes her head, and mutters, "He's just like his daddy."

So Mario chooses to go down with the deal, "One more time." he reassures himself.

It's just about 5 p.m. His music is booming as he rolls down the main street in his mint green 2006 New Edition Cadillac Escalade with 24-inch rims.

The meeting at Joe's Pancake and Waffles starts promptly at 6 p.m. Mario spots a roadblock up ahead on Main Street with the city's Red Dog Unit checking for driver's license and car insurance.

Mario thinks, "I have a valid driver's license and valid car insurance. However, the package on my back seat sure isn't valid. I had better bust a U-turn because you never know what they're going to check other than my license and car insurance. Besides, this truck is a bit too flashy for them. They'll definitely do some serious investigation."

After making the U-turn, Mario still has fifteen minutes, so he decides to take another route to Joe's Pancakes and Waffles. It's the back streets route, which means he has to drive through enemy territory. But his pride keeps telling him, "So what, I'm driving through my enemies' neighborhood. I'm Oreo! I can't be stopped."

While driving relentlessly and fearlessly, Mario approaches one of the toughest projects in America. Stopped at a red light, he pulls out his A-K47 and makes sure that it is loaded. He convinces himself, "If it's going to go down, it's just going to go down! I don't want to kill anyone but if it's necessary, I gotta do what I gotta do!"

The light turns green. Mario turns left and heads towards the projects. It is now eight minutes before six o'clock. All of a sudden, Mario looks in his rear view mirror and sees a police car behind him with its lights flashing. Mario then turns down his booming music and hears the officer through the loudspeaker, "Pull over, buddy."

In shock, Mario's first thought is, "No! I can't pull over now I have too much dirt on me!"

Then he quickly re-evaluates and says to himself, "I'll pull over. Maybe it's something minor. I know I didn't do anything." As he drops the A-K47 in a special hidden spot located in the floor of the truck he pulls over and watches the officer approach the tinted windows. The officer knocks on the window and Mario rolls it down by pushing the automatic button.

"Good evening, sir. May I have your driver's license and insurance card, please, sir."

Mario answers, "Yes, sir, you may."

"Thank you, sir. I'll be back shortly."

Mario asks the officer, "Why am I being pulled over?"

The officer replies, "Back at the traffic light, you made a left turn without turning on your signal."

"Okay, sir. But could you please hurry? I have an appointment to make within the next five minutes."

"Okay, what I'll do for you is write you out a warning citation this time, but don't let it happen again. Give me a couple of minutes to check out everything."

"Okay, officer," Mario replies.

A couple of minutes turns into twenty minutes. Mario calls the guy he was supposed to meet with at Joe's on his cell phone.

Out of frustration, "What going on?" asks the guy on the phone.

Mario answers, "Another police car just pulled up. I'll call you back. They're approaching my vehicle."

Mario quickly flips his phone closed. He knows that if he is caught, it is all over for him.

Two officers, including the one who pulled him over, came to his window.

"Mr. Mario, did you know there is a warrant out for your arrest?"

"A warrant! No way I didn't know!"

"Well, it's a four-year-old warrant. Apparently, you missed a court date. Mr. Mario, we're going to have to arrest you."

As soon as Mario hears these words, he immediately pulls away at full speed. You know what's going on now. Mario is racing through back streets trying to shake the police. He keeps saying to himself, "I can't believe I'm involved in a high-speed chase!!!"

A string of police cars pursues Mario. Sirens scream everywhere. Mario finally reaches the projects, hoping he can choose one of the narrow streets and hit one of the back alleys. Mario turns into the projects full speed, and as he looks back at the police, he hits a little girl riding on a big wheel. The little girl's flowered dress gets caught under the truck's left front tire, and she is dragged under the truck.
Mario stops the truck and jumps out as the police close in. Mario asks the girl, "Are you okay?" She just keeps screaming and crying. He tells her, "I'm sorry," then takes off down the alley running.

Mario leaves everything in the truck, including the big package. As he runs for his life he thinks, "Why did I not listen to that voice my Mama told me about!" He hits a big open field and runs as fast as he can, but a police helicopter spots him. That doesn't slow Mario down. He sees a fence at the end of the field, with a riverbank on the other side. As he glances back, he sees six police officers racing toward him.

"Freeze, I said freeze!" the officers shout.

However, Mario just climbs over the 10-foot fence. He clears the top, then slips and falls, so hard that he breaks both legs. The chase is over. Mario is arrested at 6:45 p.m.

Mario is taken to a hospital and treated. After that, he is taken to the county jail. The little girl he hit was pronounced dead at the scene. The police find the big package he was attempting to deliver at the meeting at Joe's—two kilos of crack cocaine—along with an A-K47 machine gun. Mario is charged with:

- Involuntary manslaughter
- Trafficking
- Possession of a weapon
- Reckless driving
- Attempting to elude police

Later, after a long trial, Mario was sentenced to 40 years in prison without parole. Mario's life seemed doomed. No hope, no future, and no life. Sometimes he thought of suicide, but never followed through with it, because that same voice that his mother told him to listen to told him, "Don't do it. There's hope." Though he still didn't understand the voice he was more attentive to it.

Still feeling rejected, confused insecure and anxious, Mario sat behind bars hearing the echoes of a phrase most men have heard all their lives, "You're just like your daddy!"

## Super Section Two: Don't believe the lie

No! You're are not just like your daddy. You're actually just like the one who's responsible for creating you–God. God isn't a human being. He's a spirit. And whether you know it or not, you are also a spirit, but one that happens to live in a physical body. The physical part of your body represents the flesh and your way of thinking. The flesh–your way of thinking–battles with your spirit. God anxiously waits for you to develop your spirit into a character just like Jesus. Those characteristics are the fruit of the spirit such as love, joy, peace, gentleness, faithfulness, patience, meekness, kindness and temperance. Once you adopt each characteristic and apply it to your everyday life, you'll become the powerful man God created you to be.

The question is, what is holding men back from becoming who they really are? If God wants us to be successful, why aren't we successful? Why is it we won't take care of our children? Why do we beat up our wives? Why do we keep going through the revolving door of county jails and prisons? Why are women supporting families, dominating the corporate arena and faithfully attending church? Why is "failure" tattooed on our foreheads? Why do we dream big, but never see the dream become reality? Why don't we have a vision? Why are you in so much bondage to fear? Why? Why? Why? We can go on forever and still end up with the root to all questions: *Why?*

Sometime in your life, whether you're young or old, you believed a lie Satan told you! He lied on you and said,

- "You'll never ever make it!"
- "That dream will never come true!"
- "You'll always be defeated!"
- "You'll always lose and not ever win!"
- "Your life is over, look at all the time you have wasted!"
- "You are just like your daddy–a failure!"
- "No one loves you, including God!"
- "Who's going to hire you? You don't qualify."
- "You have been to prison everyone knows that you are a low life, a nobody!"
- "Stop trying, give up! You're not going to be successful!"
- "You are a homosexual for life! There's no way out."
- "You are an addict! Drugs, sex and alcohol there's no way out!"
- Your kids and wife don't want you back!"
- "Your whole family thinks you're a wimp!"

Satan is always looking for someone to deliver his hateful lies. His main objective is to keep you from realizing Christ loves you. Satan knows how much of a threat you could become to the kingdom of darkness, which is today's world. Remember–the flesh is the way of thinking. That's where the war is, in our thinking. It's the evil thoughts that fill the arena of our mind. Once you act upon those lies, it'll produce the enemy's desired result. Well, how do we stop our flesh, our way of thinking, from signing the package of lies we've signed for all our life?

If you really are sincere about changing, I have the answer for you. If you truly want to change, you'll have to change the way you think!

Gentlemen, you are now holding and reading the material that God used to create you and the world. A book of faith-filled words designed to help you discover who you really are. Words that will line you up with what God says you are instead of the lies of the enemy spoken to you by people that were close to you, or not so close to you. Keep in mind that you must always *apply* what you read in order to obtain the desired results!

Well, it happened for Mario! Mario, who went to prison with a 40- year sentence, had a choice to make after he came into the knowledge of God. After serving only two years in prison, he was introduced to Jesus Christ by a 26- year-old man named Mr. Hambrick. Mario soon discovered who he really was in Christ. He learned that he had been living a lie all those years when people were telling him, "You are just like your daddy." He always mentioned the fact that if he had known who he really was years ago, he'd be a whole lot further in life. But Mario was very persistent in changing into who he was in Christ by changing the way he thought. Because of his trust and faithfulness in

God, God became faithful to him by honoring his word he promised him and anyone else. God's word states,

> The Lord gives freedom to the prisoners. (Psalm 146:7)

also,

> I'll restore the years the locust worm has eaten. (Joel 2:25)

After only serving five years of a 40-year sentence, Mario was released! God miraculously delivered Mario from prison and restored back to him everything that was lost, including his relationships with his seven children, in addition to producing a healthy relationship with all seven of the children's mothers. The Bible does say,

> When a man's ways please the Lord, he'll cause his enemies to shake his hand or be at peace with him.

Mario has always had an entrepreneurial spirit. That's why he was so successful with selling and distributing drugs. He was using his gift in the wrong function. Today, he owns a multi-million dollar software company. He married a beautiful woman named Candice and they have a son named Mario Jr.

What happened to all the lies? They were finally kicked out of Mario's mind. He also recognized the voice his mother told to heed. It's the voice of God.

Men, there are no more excuses, the word of God works–ask Mario! If God can do it for Mario and me, he can surely do it for you. All you need to do is what we did: discover who you really are in Christ.

READ ON TO CHAPTER THREE. IT'S TIME TO GO TO WORK!

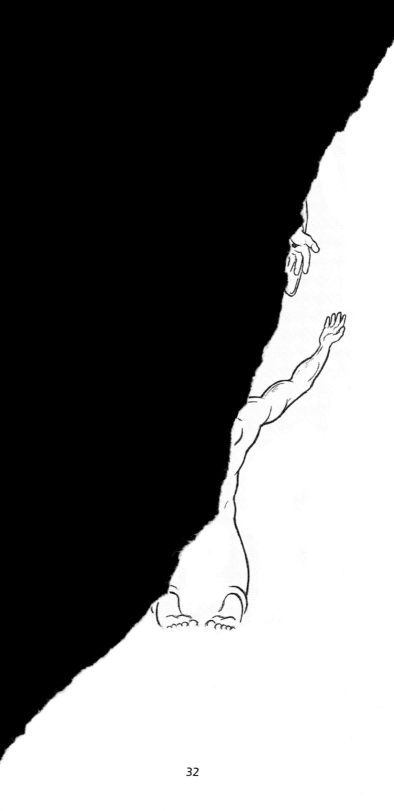

# Chapter Three

## Super Section One: "This is who you really are!"

*Then God said, "Let us make man in our image according to our likeness.*
*(Genesis 1:26)*

Were you able to see yourself in Mario? Did you say to yourself, "Hey, that same thing happened to me!" Or perhaps your life didn't demonstrate that particular pattern, but you were able to recognize a few of Mario's traits. Traits like fear, selfishness, low self-esteem or just cold hard stubbornness! Such traits and many more were rooted and grounded in Mario's heart from a young age. He grew up hearing negative messages. People told him he'd never make it. "You're just like your daddy, a deadbeat bum!" "We don't want you around–you're slow and stupid!" Throughout Mario's life, he believed the lies and the results were horrible.

What you believe about yourself is what you'll act on and eventually will become. Why? "Believe" is an action word. You'll act on what you believe about yourself whether it's positive or negative. In fact, where you are now and what you have in life is a result of what you have believed about yourself. Every human being on the planet desires to believe in something. No wonder there are so many religions in the world today. People are truly sincere about believing in something. God's desire is for people to believe in Him and in His son, Jesus Christ. It hurts God when people don't believe in him and his son. When you don't believe in God or his son, Jesus Christ, trouble always resides in your life. The Bible says in John 14:1,

*Let not your heart be troubled; you believe in God, believe also in me.*

Do you have any trouble in your life at this moment? If so, here's the answer to get it out of your life. Believe in God and his son, Jesus Christ. Look into God's word and find out what Jesus had to say about your trouble. He did say in John 14:6,

*I am the way, the truth, and the life.*

Find out Jesus' way out of your trouble. Locate Jesus' truth instead of the world's truth. When you do so, you'll find life in every area in your life.

As you already know, Mario experienced a lot of trouble in his life. I did also. I used to wonder all the time and ask myself what exactly was wrong with me! Why does negative troubled energy seem to follow me around? You could say that, in some degree, I was another Mario. I don't have a mint green Cadillac Escalade. I don't have seven children. However, I must admit I shared a wealth of Mario's characteristics like fear, insecurities and low self-esteem, and I've even gone to prison. That's right–prison! I was convicted and sentenced on October 14, 2005, to serve a year for a probation violation. I remember the day I was sentenced. I said to myself, "What a tragedy!"

I just couldn't believe I was actually going to prison! The "crime" was something so small, so petty! I was hurt and devastated. I didn't know what to expect. I had heard about prison and watched a few prison movies. I remember asking myself and other inmates in the county jail: Is it just like the movies? No way, they'd say as veteran inmates laughed. Prison is what you make of it! I truly feared the unknown.

I'll never forget arriving at River's State Prison in Hardwick, Georgia. I remember stepping off an old rundown prison bus and looking up at this big old haunted Frankenstein-looking building. After they processed me, I went outside into the yard and saw hundreds of men playing basketball, smoking cigarettes and arguing. It was a sea of white, black, Hispanic and Asian men. I'd never seen so many different races of men in one place. As I walked around the yard with my hands in my pockets and a perplexed look, older men would approach me and say, "Hey, kid, what are you here for?" I'd say because of this and that. They'd say, "What! They sent you to prison because of that!" "Yes, sir," I'd reply. "Well, how much time did they give you?" I'd say, "One year." "What! You only have one year!" as they laughed.

Keep in mind, I was speaking with men who'd been in a chain gang anywhere from 15 to 40 years. Some guys were serving life sentences. After I continued to explore my new home, I saw some unbelievable things that you only hear about. Experiencing it was entirely different. This included homosexuality. Men were kissing, holding hands, laying their heads on each other's shoulders, and even had sex with each other. They were known as "Sissies." They included the prison's church choir director, who performed oral sex throughout the week. It all blew my mind!

Did I look down on the guys? NO! I didn't! Why? I knew God loved them, but hated what they did. I met men from all walks of life. I knew in my heart that I could help them. I knew I could deliver them with

34

the word of God, thanks to the guidance and teaching of my spiritual father and pastor, Creflo A. Dollar, Jr. However, before I could help them, I had to find out what was actually wrong with *me*. I began looking around the dorm for a place I could get in touch with God. It was very difficult to do that with 80 men in one big dorm room. I managed to find a spot. However, it was a very uncomfortable spot, known as "The Shack." This was a small room where men committed unspeakable sins. I'd wait until 4 or 5 in the morning or between the hours of 1 and 8 p.m. I was out of the way at night. That's when others did their thing. After being there for a while, that little room became my office. I used a red cooler for a chair. Other men began respecting me. They knew I was in there to either pray or study the word of God. Men would always come in for prayer or join in on a little Bible study. That place was transformed from "The Shack" to the "Word Shack."

I was in search of what was going on with me. After seeking God about what was wrong with me, he began to tell me. He said, "Keith, the reason why you have had so much trouble in your life is because of two reasons. One, you have believed all of the lies that Satan has told you ever since your youth, and two, you don't know who you really are in Christ." Bingo! By spending time in the presence of God, I received the answer to every problem that I had. Keith Brooks simply didn't know who he was in Christ! In addition, because he didn't know who he was in Christ, he believed every negative word that came from his stepfather, coach, and family and friends that the enemy used.

After God told me my hang-ups, I asked him what to do now. He said, "There are three things that you must do while you have time to serve in prison:

- Develop in love, become a man of love.
- Get rid of fear.
- Find out who you are in Christ.

After spending a year with Creflo A. Dollar himself, you'd think any man would be a completely changed man. Rightfully so, he would if he applied what he learned. I had all of this knowledge and word invested inside me that was just there lying dormant. As I began to do what God had instructed me to do, I began to remember and understand what Pastor Dollar had taught me in The Joseph Project (a mentorship program). Everything seemed to be clicking. Every principle, confession, and the law of life I was taught from Creflo Dollar was standing on the foundation of the word of God.

Nothing can compare to spending time with God. When you make a quality decision out of hunger for the word of God, that's when God will make a quality decision in revealing his precious jewels to you. My main objective was to discover who I really am in Christ Jesus. This is one of the jewels that God had placed in me at my new birth, born again experience. I'm about to share with you what God shared with me. So grab your Bible, pen, highlighter and some paper, and open your heart as I pour the rich, good news of who you really are into your life so you can become the supernatural hero that you **actually are.**

Did you know that you are just like God? Did you know you were made in His image? "What! How could you say such a thing? You must be a false prophet!" you may say. It's okay, if you did say something like this. I have the word of God to back me up, to prove to you that this is who you really are. Open your Bible to Genesis 1:26 where it states,

*Then God said, "Let us make man in our image, according to our likeness.*

Did you see that! I didn't say that–God said it! In addition, he said it about you! You see the first step to recognizing "who you really are" is knowing that God created you in His own image. It would be so nice to know where you really came from, wouldn't you agree? You may say, "I came from my mother and father." That is completely true to a certain extent. No man or woman can enter this planet without coming through the womb of a woman first. Allow me to ask you this, "Who created your mother and father?" Who is it that actually causes a sperm cell and egg cell to collide with one another and form little fingers, toes and bones?" Scientists couldn't even tell you that! The root to all creation is God; that's his M.O. He's very creative. He has the ability to open his mouth and create things. And God said, "Let there be light." And God said, "Let there be water." And God said, "Let there be grass." And God said, "Let the person that's reading this book be made in my image and in my likeness." In other words, I created you to be just like me. Look now at Genesis 1:1-31 and underline every verse that starts out by saying *God said*, and when you approach verse 31 you'll see that God saw everything that he said! Did you know you could see what you say? That's one of your super powers. That's who you really are, a speaking spirit. So, if you have been speaking failure, fear-filled words, begin speaking successful, faith-filled words. The Bible says in Proverbs 18:21,

*Death and life is in the power of the tongue.*

Begin to speak life, which is the word of God, over your family, finances, debt, any bondage, over your future, and the dreams that you have. Speak the word of God, like God did. Speak over the situation that you're standing in right now. Begin to say, "It's not over! God is going to get me out! I'll no longer lose! I am going to be victorious! I am a superhero. I can't be stopped!" Begin to say, "I am just like God and I am made in His image!"

Now please understand that everything has a power switch, an on and off button. For example, let's look at a light switch–you can switch it on and off, but if that light switch does not have any power flowing to it, it's useless! When God opens his mouth, he speaks with power. Here's another question, "What is the power? What is God's power? What is the power that turns on the lights? Electricity! Likewise, God's power is his word! And the switch is his mouth. Now think with me for a moment. If God's power is his word and the switch is his mouth, and you are made just like him. That ought to tell you that the word of God is *your* power and the switch is *your* mouth. Put the word inside of you, dump the word of God into your heart and when you open your mouth, which is your switch, the power will flow out! The Bible says in Luke 6:45,

*For out of the abundance of the heart the mouth speaks.*

Whatever situations you're facing or circumstance you're dealing with, open the word of God, find your "power food bars" (scriptures) and eat them! So when you open your mouth, the power will be released to destroy any problem in your life. For example, if you need healing in or on your physical body, open God's word, your power source, and look up healing "power food bars" (scriptures) and eat them. Get them in your heart, open your mouth and then speak healing over your physical body. This will work for anything: deliverance from drug addictions, alcohol addictions, sexual addictions, homosexuality, AIDS and other diseases, fear, worry, anger and suicidal thoughts.

The word of God will also heal your finances, marriage, and relationships. You are just like God; begin to act like it's already so in your life–that's faith! Begin to practice your super powers. This is who you really are! A man created in the image of God, made in God's likeness. You can win in life. You'll win in life and know that superheroes never fail. They always end up with the victory.

# Super Section Two: "Did he steal your identity?"

"I wanna be Batman! Hey, look at me! I'm going to climb this tree just like Spiderman climbed up that building that was on fire to save that little old lady."

"Now son, you might not want to pick up that box; it is a little too heavy for you." "But, Mama, watch this. I'm strong like the Incredible Hulk!"

Can you recall when you were a child saying these same phrases? Then you became a teenager and grew a little older, so you made statements such as, "I'm going to be the next Michael Jordan!"

"No one will be able to play and save the team by making the game winning shot like I can."

"I'm the baddest fighter in my school and neighborhood. I'm the next Mike Tyson."

"I am another Tupac. No one can beat me rapping."

"Yeah! They said I was just like my daddy, I guess they were right because I am a smooth dude when it comes to pimping the women. People come to me and buy my dope and other drugs. Why? Because I have the best there is in town. I'll soon take over the world. I'll be just like another Scarface!"

Now that you're an adult, you tend to think you have got it all together and no one can tell you anything! You're shining like a fresh coat of metallic paint on a car, which only cost you one hundred and fifty dollars. Or, how about that glossy furniture you purchased. It was cheap but looked so expensive. Things and people who quickly shine always end up fading out. How about shining in the inside first instead of just on the outside? For example, the reason why the fresh, metallic paint job on the car faded was because the car wasn't properly sanded down. It was just completely painted. Oh, and what happened to the legs of that beautiful, glossy table? Well, the legs had unseen cracks in them and just happened to be painted over with a high gloss coat of paint. So when a buyer came in to purchase the table, it quickly sold because of the high gloss, expensive look. However, after a couple of months, the table wasn't able to stand! Why? Because the buyer couldn't see what was inside the legs of the table, which was the "cracks." He or she paid attention to the outside instead of the inside.

Images, images and images: How do you see yourself? When we were little boys, we saw ourselves as superheroes and then when we became teenagers, we saw ourselves as great sports athletes. We had a contest with other guys to see how many phone numbers we could get from the girls. Then we became young men desiring to become the biggest dope dealer all the way to becoming the CEO of a huge company. But what's actually causing these desires to appear in the lives of men whether they are negative or positive?

Images! Where you are today could be a result of the image that you carried around within yourself. There is absolutely nothing wrong with images as long as they are positive. When you were a kid, you imagined you were a superhero and there was nothing wrong with that. In fact, that's the point of this book. It's about locating and awakening the superhero inside of you! In every man, there lies a superhero. Our women are looking for heroes. Your community is looking for heroes. On the job, they are looking for heroes. In your state, at your church, and your children are looking for heroes. Your family is looking for a hero. The whole globe is looking for a superhero who not only knows how to demonstrate his powers but demonstrate the source of his power, which is love. We'll talk more on that as you read along.

As you have already read, you are made in the image of God and in his likeness. You have the same power God has—it is consecrated inside of you. The moment you received Jesus Christ as Lord and Savior over your life, God's son then invested his power inside of you! It's been there ever since you became a Christian. It has been waiting for you to tap into it. There are many super powers that God has given you, to help you become a hero in other people's eyes. One super power we discovered in the first section of this chapter was the power of speaking words. The next super power is the power of imagination, in short ,"image." So, if God is the foundation of our super powers, let's find out what he said about our imagination. Look with me in your Bible at Genesis 11:1-6,

*Now the whole earth had one language and one speech. And it came to pass, as they journeyed form the east that they found a plain in the land of Shinar, and they dwelt there. Then they said to one another, "Come, let us make bricks and bake them thoroughly." They had brick for stone, and they had asphalt for mortar. In addition, they said, "Come, let us build ourselves a city, and a tower whose top is in the heavens, lest we be scattered abroad over the face of the whole earth." But the Lord came down to see the city and the tower which the sons of men had built. And the Lord said, "Indeed the people are one and they all have one language, and this is what they begin to do; Now nothing that they imagine to do will be withheld from them.*

Wow! That's powerful. Did you just see that? Here, you had people who decided to come together in one accord, and they all put their God-given power–which was their imagination—together, and they imagined building a tower that could break through the floor of heaven. God himself had to come down and stop them by confusing their language. He said, "If I don't stop these people, nothing will be able to restrain, stop or be withheld from them when they make a decision to operate in their power of imagination." Not only did they imagine it, but they spoke with words also! Even God imagined a blue sky before he spoke it. He imagined the water being blue instead of pink. He imagined the dirt, grass, and animals and spoke them into existence. He imagined you and spoke you into existence. Remember, he made you in his image and in his likeness. You have the same kind of imagination that God has and you can speak out what you imagine into existence! Please see what God is trying to show you! You, man of God, have super powers! Will you please come out of the telephone booth with your head up, back straight,, with your fists on your hips equipped with the super powers of God? Are you ready to attack the emergencies of life such as debt, divorce, generational curses, poverty, sickness and disease, and every other curse that's controlling the lives of people, including yours? Men, the time is now! Time is running out! You are going to have to make a decision and use what God has given you. It is the only way that you are going to see supernatural results in your life.

Now let's deal with something. Ask yourself these questions:

- Why have I been failing?
- Why has my business been failing?
- Why is my marriage not working, now facing divorce?
- Why am I not married?
- Why haven't my dreams come true yet?
- Why am I so fearful?
- Why does everyone else seem to prosper instead of me?
- Why is my whole life shattered like broken glass?
- Why me? Why me? Why me?

Gentlemen, please understand that you are not the only man on the planet that says with a heavy heart, *Why me?* However, there is a cause to every negative thing that happens in your life and the same with every positive thing that happens in your life. The question you need to ask yourself is, *What is causing me to fail?* Period. You may be saved, sanctified and filled with the Holy Ghost. You may do many good deeds as a Christian and tell everyone that you are righteous because of what you do and there isn't anything wrong with that. Keep that zeal to do good. But good deeds are not enough when you are still failing in life! Far too many men experience the pain of failure instead of the joy of victory.

The world (which could be your family members or friends) may say, "Why should I become a Christian when you are doing just as bad or even worse than I am?" Such statements hurt, but could be true. In fact, the Bible mentions that the world is looking for strong Christian men who have results in their life. Look with me at Romans 8:19 ,

*For the earnest expectation of the creation eagerly waits for the revealing of the sons of God.*

Men, can you see how important it is for the sons of God to live a successful Christian lifestyle? Although your coworkers might appear happy and your old buddies may seem successful, that's not always the case. Although they appear to shine like a fresh paint job or glow like the glossy coat that covers the defective wooden table, they're hurting on the inside and looking for answers. This is why the manifestations of God's goodness should be flowing out of your life. Could it be that they are waiting to see the revealing of a successful Christian lifestyle from you? Of course they are! Yet we are being defeated with failure after failure. "Why?" is the question that needs answering. Look with me at Psalm 11:3,

Remember, you are righteous because you accepted Jesus as Lord of your life. And if you don't have Jesus Christ in your life, I'd recommend that you receive him as Lord over your life instead of keeping the world as Lord over your life, which will cause you confusion, pain and death.

You still may ask yourself, "Am I righteous?" (which means right standing with God). But there's no evidence in my life that I am righteous. The very reason why there's failure in your life is because your foundation is destroyed. "What is the foundation?" you ask. The weak foundation that you have is the fact that you don't know who you really are! Yep! That's it! Well, I'm a good police officer or I'm a great teacher, or I'm one of the best ushers in my church. That's all fine and good, but we're not focusing on what you *do*, we're focusing on who you really *are*. You can lose your job tomorrow and still be faced with the reality of who you really are. The number one foundation of a man's life is his relationship with God. Once you establish a relationship with God through reading and meditating on his word (the Holy Bible) you'll soon begin to discover your true identity. A man with constant failure in his life is a man who constantly does not know who he really is. Remember there's a cause to everything that you do. What's causing you not to know who you are? Not spending time with the word of God. What's getting more of your attention than the word of God, which will show you who you really are? And who's causing you not to give yourself a chance to discover who you really are?

It's Satan himself, who comes to kill, steal and destroy. Did he steal your true identity? One of Satan's devices that he has used on men over the years and still uses today is a false image of what a man is. He has used this device ever since a male child was born, became a teenager, then grew to a full-grown man. Many men grew up wanting to be like someone else. Some didn't because they were mature enough to find themselves. However, those who have suffered from not knowing who they are usually had a verbally and physically abusive past.

God uses people to encourage, inspire, and motivate others, Satan uses people to discourage, condemn, and curse others but he uses devices such as stepfathers, hurt and confused mothers, teachers, coaches, and others that are close to you. Their job was to plant a false self-image in you that appeared real to you. Notice I said *appeared* because whenever Satan speaks, he lies. Lies such as, "Give it up, you'll never make it! You are going to fail just like your daddy. You have a very slim chance of making it because you are not very smart. You are not quite that talented. The odds are against you. You are ugly. You are weak. You are so fat. You'll never lose weight. You are so dumb and stupid. You are very slow. You don't comprehend well."

Men that suffer from a poor self-image at an early age and throughout manhood tend to look for other images to be like. For example, the biggest dope dealer in the city, the hard-core gangsta rapper, the rock star that will do anything–role models that are sometimes dishing out false images themselves.

Not all role models are bad. I'm only speaking about the ones who purposefully are sending out negative messages and vibes. While I was in prison, I met a young man who murdered another young man. After talking with him on how it went down, I soon wanted to know the root of why he did what he did. He said, "I thought I was just like this rapper because he rapped about if someone does you wrong you shoot them and kill them so I did just that." Music is one of the biggest influences on the planet today and the artists, whether they are gangsta rap or a rock and roller, really don't live the way they sing or rap. It's a false image that they provide to the listener to make money, but the listener begins to do what he's listening to, acts on it and finds himself in trouble while the music entertainer is on a beach somewhere sipping on some lemonade. Can you see how Satan uses his devices to steal your true identity, to keep you from knowing who you are? Can you see how dangerous it is to follow a false image? Have you realized how important it is to know who you are? Men that don't know who they are always operate under the flesh, which produces Galatians 5:19-2–turn there and read with me,

> *Now the works of the flesh are evident, which are: adultery, fornication, uncleanness, lewdness, idolatry, sorcery, hatred, contentions, jealousies, outbursts of wrath, selfish ambitions, dissensions, heresies, envy, murders, drunkenness, revelries (wild parties), and the like; of which I tell you beforehand, just as I have also told you in time past, that those who practice such things shall not inherit the kingdom of God.*

Now that's a serious list of devices that Satan uses in the lives of men today. They are the works of the flesh. However, what's causing a man to do those works? Simple! Not knowing who you are! Look at that list again. Can you locate yourself in that list? Are you in adultery? Do you struggle with fornication, idolatry, hatred or an outburst of anger? Do you practice sorcery, have jealousies, or hold selfish ambitions? I remember when I suffered from a high dose of being insecure (which means you're not secure in yourself), and not being secure in myself equaled to not knowing who I really was in Christ. I'd just demolish relationships. I was about to marry the woman of my dreams but ended up chasing her away from me as far as the east to the west, by practicing some of Satan's devices, including jealousy and envy. I'd say, look at that guy's truck–his truck looks better than my little 1989 Buick Century, or, look at his muscles–he thinks he's Hercules. Then I'd turn around and accuse my girlfriend of wanting the guy whose muscles were bigger than mine or whose vehicle was better looking than my little hoopty! We'd go into restaurants and I couldn't enjoy my meal because I'd assume that every guy that walked past our table she'd like more than me because he looked better than me or had a nicer suit than I was wearing. She couldn't enjoy her meal because I'd accuse her every five minutes. It wasn't until she left me that I realized that she wanted me, not for who I wasn't or for what I had. She had seen the potential that I had and the anointing that rested on my life. Always remember that assumption is the lowest form of knowledge. Insecurity, jealousy, anger and the rest of the fruits of the flesh are all fear-based. For everything that was stated in Galatians 5:19-21, fear is the foundation. Take anger, for example. It seems as though 85% of the men in today's world are affected with anger. Why? Because they don't know who they are. They are rooted and grounded in fear. Here's a scenario. Jacob comes home from work and soon as he walks through the door his two kids, a girl and a boy, run as fast as they can and wrap themselves around their father's legs, excited to see him. His beautiful wife, wearing a touch of Jacob's favorite perfume, follows the children. She announces that she's made Jacob's favorite meal of roast beef and potatoes with macaroni and cheese and a big slice of carrot cake to go with it. As she goes to Jacob, he snatches his kids off of his legs, orders them to go to their room, pushes his wife off of him and storms into their bedroom and slams the door behind him! After ten minutes or so, the wife gently walks into the bedroom and asks her husband, "What's wrong with you? Why are you so angry?" He then says, "I'm afraid that I'm about to be laid off from my job because we have a lack of work. And how are the bills going to get paid?" We see what Jacob is angry about. But have you located the root of his anger? That's right–fear! The fear of losing his job and not being able to pay the bills is what's making Jacob angry. And when you're angry, you fear something, and when you operate in fear, you don't know who you are! Ask yourself this question, "What am I fearing when I get angry?" When you don't know who you are in Christ, you then are under Satan's device called fear.

I believe now you may have a clear understanding of why there's failure in your life or even the fact of not knowing who you are in Christ. When your foundation is destroyed, what can you do? Did Satan steal your identity by blinding you with false images and negative emotions? If so, there's nothing but good news ahead as you continue to read the upcoming chapters. But we must keep first things first and that's to build a new foundation on who we really are in Christ. As we are continuing to build the new foundation, let's look at the first man that was created by God and let's investigate how Satan stole that man's true identity. God loves you so much that one of the purposes for the Bible was to give you examples of other people in the Bible who failed and then had victories. Men of God, put up a fight against the devices of Satan! Without a fight there could be no victory! In addition, the first step in training for those fights and obtaining your superhero abilities is to discover who you really are. As you continue to read, you'll hear God speaking to your heart as he says this is who you really are!

# Super Section Three: A defeated superhero

Whatever God creates, it's super. Another word for super is anointed. The word *anointed* is the burden-removing, yoke-destroying power of God. Physically you are a natural man. However, when God anoints you, you become a supernatural man—a man that removes burdens and destroys yokes. What good is it just to be a natural man? What good would Superman be if he lost his super powers? What good would Batman be without his utility belt? What good would Spiderman be without his ability to shoot out spider webs or how about the Incredible Hulk not having access to his strength? They would all be defeated superheroes if they were not able to demonstrate their super powers in any circumstance or in any situation that life brought them.

The very first man God created was a superhero. This man was created in the image of God, God's anointing was on his natural physical body, which caused him to become a supernatural man. Adam had super abilities running through him just like electricity runs through an extension cord. God gave Adam power to dominate, to rule and reign as a king throughout the whole earth. Look with me at Genesis 1:28

*Then God blessed them, and God said to them, "Be fruitful and multiply: Fill the earth and subdue it: have dominion over the fish of the sea, over the birds of the air, and over every living thing that moves on the earth."*

Notice that at the beginning of that scripture it says that God blessed them! Did you know that God was talking about you and me? That's right—he was talking to the men. He told Adam and you and me to be fruitful and multiply, fill the earth and subdue it, and to have dominion over every living thing that moves on the earth! Now that's super power!!

Whenever God anoints a man, it is usually for a specific purpose or an assignment. He did exactly that with Adam. Look at Genesis 2:19-20,

*Out of the ground the Lord God formed every beast of the field and every bird of the air, and brought them to Adam to see what he'd call them. And whatever Adam called each living creature, that was its name. So Adam gave names to all cattle, to the birds of the air, and to every beast of the field.*

Isn't it amazing to know the animals that we see today are the same animals that Adam gave names to? That was a part of his assignment. What a huge assignment, to name every beast, bird, fish, and creeping thing (insect). This assignment might have looked huge in our eyes but not in Adam's. Why? Because Adam was given the super power to get the assignment accomplished. Adam was anointed by God to carry out anything that God ordered him to do. God had given Adam the whole earth. He was the God of the earth! God gave him the super power to dominate in every arena in the earth. But here's a question for you, "What is your assignment?" Do you know? Why has God on purpose created you? Why has God on purpose placed you on the earth?

Many men waste many years trying to discover their purpose in life. Whether you are a Christian or not, this has to be one of the biggest concerns in the mind of a man. What has God called me to do? I asked others and myself religiously! It wasn't until I found my calling that I questioned why I asked everybody what my calling was instead of asking the very source of my calling. I remember trying to be this or that. I remember trying to be like someone else because I didn't like myself.

A man will always be frustrated in life until he locates what he's been created to do. For example, you take a fish out of a fish bowl and throw it on the ground; it will wiggle, waggle, and flop, gasping for water. But why is the fish so frustrated? Because the fish wasn't created to live on the ground! He was created to swim. But if you pick that fish up before it dies and place it back into the fish bowl, it will be the most fascinating thing to watch. Why? The fish is fulfilling its purpose.

Are you frustrated? Do you find yourself throughout life wiggling and waggling, suffering from depression, suicidal thoughts, hopelessness, insecurity, anxiety, and poverty? If so, your struggle isn't really those things. Your struggle will always be found in the foundation of your life and not knowing who you really are. Say to yourself, "If I am frustrated and confused, I must focus all of my attention and energy in finding out who I am. You may ask, "How can I know what my calling is?" And that's a good question because God never intended for you to walk around in the dark. There are three solid ways to locate your calling.

*Spend a lot of time in the word of God.* As you begin to read and find out who you are, your foundation will begin to form, shaping you into a man of God. And once you begin to form in his image by putting what you learned about yourself in your heart. God then sees and says, "That man is ready for me to reveal his purpose." Just think–you are only in Chapter Two in this book and have read and realized parts of who you are! You know that you are a speaking spirit. You can speak things into existence just like God can. You also know that your imagination is a very powerful tool. You understand that whatever you imagine doing, you can't be stopped! Spending time in the word of God is spending time with him.

*Name what it is that you love to do.* Most of the time your gift is wrapped up in your calling. What is the thing that you love to do so much that you don't have to be paid for it? This thing is your passion! Also begin to ask others, "What am I good at? Asking others that are close to you, people who know you and have been around you, "What am I good or gifted in?" will be a good way to locate your gift that will support your calling. Remember to ask those who will be honest with you.

Adam was the ultimate superhero! God gave him the power to dominate and to win in life. I mean this guy couldn't lose in anything; there was no failure in Adam. He never even heard of the word failure! Adam had an assignment and put his whole heart into what God called him to do! He was focused and as he was busy doing what God called him to do, God gave him a wife, a helpmeet. She, Eve, became one with Adam, doing what God called him to do. Do you desire to have a wife? If yes, begin to do what Adam did. Find out who you really are. Locate your calling and get busy! As you do, your helpmeet will come along desiring to become one with you. Why? She sees a man with a vision who is on a mission. But what really stands out about you is the fact that she sees the anointing. Women love characteristics of a hero! Every woman is waiting for some superman to come sweep her off her feet.

The time will come, as you begin to walk in your calling, for that special helpmate to join you in the assignment that God has for you. It is very important if you are single to position yourself, like a baseball catcher positions himself, to receive the pitch from the pitcher. "How do I position myself for my assignment, wife and all the rich blessings that God has for me?" you may ask. Find out who you really are that's how! But don't turn around and become a defeated superhero! Adam became a defeated superhero. How did Adam lose his super powers or the anointing on his life? He disobeyed God's commandment. You may or may not know the story that God had told Adam not to eat any fruit from the tree of life. Later, Adam told his God-given wife not to eat any fruit from the tree of life or she would surely die (spiritual death). One day, while Adam and Eve were working their assignment, Satan came by in the form of a walking snake and, in Genesis 3:4-7,

*Then the serpent said to the woman. "You won't surely die. For God knows that in the day you eat of it your eyes will be opened, and you will be like God, knowing good and evil." So when the woman saw that the tree was good for food, that is was pleasant to the eyes, and a tree desirable to make one wise, she took off its fruit and ate. She also gave to her husband with her, and he ate. Then the eyes of both of them were opened, and they knew that they were naked; and they sewed fig leaves together and made themselves coverings.*

Can you see how Satan deceived Adam and Eve? If you look in verse six, you'll see that she gave to her husband with her and he ate. So, if Adam was with her and heard the words coming out of Satan's mouth, why didn't Adam step up and rebuke Satan to stop the lies that he was telling Eve? Because he understood that by eating the fruit from the tree he'd be like God, and that the fruit was pleasant to the eyes. Man of God, I have another question for you. Do you want to know another reason why you're living a life of failure? It is because of Satan's lies in the temptations of life. Satan may have not come in the form of a snake when he lied and caused you to fall for your temptations. He formed himself into other people, TV, movies, etc. He lied and told Adam and Eve that if they ate the fruit they'd be just like God. Why did they fall for that lie when they were already just like God? Remember, God made man in his image and in his likeness. The Bible goes on to say in verse seven that when they ate the fruit, their eyes opened and they realized they were naked! Whenever you allow sin to control your life because of the fact that you don't know who you really are, you become and feel naked which basically means the anointing is gone. The super has disappeared from your natural physical body; you are now a defeated superhero.

Adam lost it all, even his right to dominate! He could have dominated Satan when he was tempted, but he gave in to what *appeared* to look good. When God asked Adam what he had done, Adam responded in Genesis 3:12,

*Then the man said, "The woman whom you gave to be with me, she gave me of the tree, and I ate.*

Excuses, excuses–they are one of Satan's "gifts" to men who don't know who they really are. Remember, Adam could have used his super power of dominion to dominate the enemy and his lies. What excuses are you maintaining that cause you to live an unsuccessful life? Stop the excuses! Well, the white man's holding me back. The black man is holding me back. I'm not going to try to go further in my life because I have a lack of education. I'm not smart enough. I'm not talented enough. Nobody likes me. I've been to prison. I have three felonies on my record. I hurt my back so I can't work. I beat up my wife because she makes me mad. I have to sell drugs because no one will hire me.

Men, you are better than this! Stop the excuses. Take advantage of the word of God and this book. They'll guide you into locating who you really are in Christ. Adam really messed up for us all. The Bible calls his mistake the fall of man. Can you see how Satan came along and stole Adam's identity and sucked all of Adam's power by snatching the very keys to life? Because of this fall, men are born into sin and iniquity. Look at Psalm 51:5:

*Behold, I was brought forth in iniquity, and in sin my mother conceived me.*

Because of the fall, men have to sweat in their labor. (You don't have to sweat as much when you're in your calling.) Because of the fall, women have to labor with great pain during childbirth. Because of the fall, Satan has dominion on the earth and the ground is cursed. Because of the fall, fear was introduced to the world. But despite Adam's fall, what now? Good question with a good answer. God had another plan. He had to find himself another Adam, someone who could be on earth and stand up to sin and its temptations and dominate by using his power. His ultimate plan was to get the keys of his power back to mankind, which includes you and me. As you know, Satan stole the keys from Adam and was literally destroying God's earth and his creation. Now as God was looking for candidates to secure the keys back from Satan, he found someone that he had chosen to make way for his ultimate plan, from Abraham, Moses, David and Joseph to his very own son, Jesus Christ.

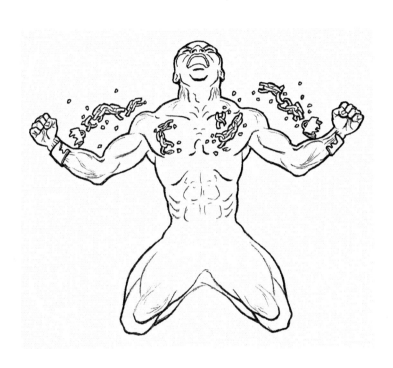

# Chapter Four

## Super Section One: Knowing your rights, your way to freedom.

*Awake to righteousness, and don't sin; for some don't have the Knowledge of God. (1 Corinthians 15:34)*

"Praise God! Praise God! Praise God, Church! Clap your hands and give God thanks and the glory for his awesome healing and deliverance power. Did you receive your healing tonight?"

"Yes!" The membership of 7,000 shouted out back to their bold and energetic pastor. This had been one powerful miracle and healing service this month! People were delivered from their wheelchairs, the lame began to walk, and people were delivered from bondages such as drugs, cigarettes, alcohol, and pornography. Lastly, but definitely not least did you see when I laid my hands on the forty-six-year-old blind man! He received his sight instantly! Why? Because he had faith that God could open his blinded eyes and believe in me by allowing me to lay hands on him, which God used my hands as a vehicle for healing."

After closing remarks, the whole church gave Pastor Shoemaker a standing ovation, as members shouted out, "We love you Pastor! You're the best!"

"Thank you, thank you and God bless you all. I also want to remind you, and especially our first-time visitors that came and fellowshipped with us tonight, that we always have these miracle and deliverance services once a month. So make sure you mark your calendar for September 8, as it will be our next miracle and deliverance service. So please, by all means, come expecting to receive your miracle. God bless you all. Have a good night. Drive home safely and I'll be seeing you soon."

Pastor Shoemaker was a man on the move for God. He was known all over the world. As pastor of "The God Church," he had started out with only two members–his wife and himself. They stepped out into the ministry a little over twenty-six years ago. With a faithful commitment to God, God had begun to prosper them and their ministry. Pastor Shoemaker had a very close relationship with a longtime friend. They both knew each other before Pastor Shoemaker married his beautiful wife. Boy, did they go through a lot together. There were many ups and downs. Pastor Shoemaker's parents both died in a devastating train crash when they were on their way to visit him at the Bible College that he attended. When the Shoemakers' friend survived a very bad divorce after being married for eight years, they still maintained a strong relationship throughout the years.

Pastor Shoemaker and his friend always shared their dreams with each other. As for Pastor Shoemaker, his dream manifested itself before his very eyes, but for his friend things didn't go so well because of procrastination and fear! He was not willing to step out, take a risk, or take chances. But because of the goodness of Pastor Shoemaker's heart, he gave his close friend an administrative position at the church. Shoemaker's friend had always been smart, intelligent, and very computer literate. His friend could also speak very well and got along well with others.

However, Pastor Shoemaker had a well-kept secret. He knew that he could perform any kind of sexual activity with his friend and his close friend felt the same way about him. After church services were over on Sundays, and after Tuesday night Bible Studies, Pastor Shoemaker would send his wife and kids home with security while he and his head administrator (his friend) stayed after for counseling sessions, meetings, etc.

On one particular Tuesday evening after Bible Study, Pastor Shoemaker and his friendly administrator were in his office discussing plans for the September 8 Miracle and Deliverance service. In the middle of the discussion, Pastor interrupted his friend and said, "Listen, pardon my interruption, but there's something that I have been thinking about for a long time and it's been hovering around in my heart for years."

His friend replied, "Okay, let's hear it!"

Pastor Shoemaker then responded, "For a very long time I have been extremely attracted to you and if I wasn't married I'd just love to have the chance to make love to you and have the opportunity to experience something different. If you're shocked about what just came out of my mouth I'm sorry, but that's just the way I feel about you."

Pastor Shoemaker's friend said, "I'm not shocked at all. You see, Pastor, I have always felt the same way about you. I've always wanted to have a lovely experience with you also, but I never made an attempt because I didn't want to disrespect you or your wife. This is why I didn't show upon your wedding day. I was angry with you and her because I wanted you for myself and I knew that I couldn't have you!" They grabbed each other's hand and looked into each other's eyes.

"Come on, big boy, show me what you got." The pastor's friend began to rub his arms and chest while unbuttoning his shirt. At that point, Pastor Shoemaker was in awe and several questions ran through his mind such as, "What will happen if my wife found out about this? What if my church found out about this? I know what I'm doing is wrong and God isn't pleased with this."

Then Pastor Shoemaker's friend said, "Come on, no one will know. This will be our secret. It's just me and you, pastor."

They began to kiss each other, touching intensified, and they began to have sexual intercourse. As this was all occurring, there was a terrible thunderstorm going on outside. It was so bad that it knocked out the electricity on the north side on the city, where Pastor Shoemaker and his family lived. First Lady Shoemaker had gathered up their two children and left the church after Tuesday night Bible Study. She arrived home and tried to open the electric gate with the gate opener inside her car. She realized the power was out and then got out the car and used her key to open the gate. When she turned the key, it broke. "Shucks!" First Lady Shoemaker said. She got back into the car, picked up her cell phone and tried to locate her husband, but she couldn't get through because the battery had died out. Not only was she facing these minor problems, but she also had two children in the back seat. One was saying, "Mommy, I'm hungry," another saying, "Mommy, I have to go to the bathroom," and they both were frightened by the storm.

The church was only fifteen minutes away and she knew that her husband was going to be at the church most of the night taking care of ministry business (at least that's what she thought). She drove back to the church to get the spare key from Pastor Shoemaker's desk. When she arrived back at the church, she saw her husband's car and his friend's vehicle parked next to each other. She rushed the kids into the church and got them situated. She gave them a snack from the church kitchen and turned on the television, so they could watch a DVD of an episode of Bibleman.

"I'll be back. I'm going up stairs to your father's office to get the key and I'll be right back."

"Okay, Mommy." they said. "Oh, Mommy before you go, can you tell daddy to come here? I'm still scared of the storm."

She said, "Okay, honey. Ha, ha...."

As First Lady Shoemaker climbed the stairs, she noticed it was very dark in the hallway leading to her husband's office. Now Pastor Shoemaker and his friend were still in his office having sex. He had also turned on some smooth jazz tunes. Pastor Shoemaker loved smooth jazz. He'd always play it just to relax from the hustle and bustle of ministry work. As First Lady Shoemaker was walking down the dark hallway, she sensed that something wasn't right. Upon hearing her and her husband's favorite jazz track, she smiled and said within herself, "Let me get my big teddy bear out of this office and get him home so that we can have a little activity. After all, it's been a while." (That's what she thinks!)

She punched in the code to open the office door, opened the door, walked in, looked to the left and screamed, "Oh, my God! Oh, my God! Earl Shoemaker and Carl, what are you guys doing? Oh no! Oh no! This can't be happening."

"Honey when did you get here?" Pastor Earl asked.

"I can't believe you, Earl. How could you be having sex with another man?"

She fell to her knees devastated, screaming and crying. One minute Pastor Earl Shoemaker loved Carl and the next minute it all turned into hate!!!

"Get out of here, Carl, and I mean now!"

Mrs. Shoemaker stood up and shouted, "It's over! It's over!"

After Pastor Shoemaker had slipped on his pants, he ran over to his wife. She spun around and ran down the hall to the staircase with her husband running after her.

"Honey, Honey! Please come back! Listen, please! Honey, I'm sorry!"

As First Lady Shoemaker ran down the stairs, she broke a heel off of her black shoe ,fell and bumped her head as she landed. However, that didn't stop her. She grabbed the kids and left. All Pastor Shoemaker could do was fall to his knees and cry out to God saying, "God please forgive me! Will you please forgive me?"

When he returned home he found a note on the bed that read,

Earl,

I cannot believe you. I didn't know that you were gay and neither did I know that Carl was a homosexual! It's over! I don't want you anymore. I trusted you. I really did. Don't bother me. I need time to think.

The kids and I are headed to Philadelphia to my mom and dad's house.

—Karen

Pastor Shoemaker stood all alone in his $2.5 million dollar home. He had lost the thing that was most precious to him and blocked the thing that was most valuable to him–God's presence, the anointing, and the very power of God. Now, did God take away his calling as a minister? Of course not, because the Bible says that the gifts and callings of God are without repentance. This means that whatever God gives you, he'll never take away. The only way that it can go away is if you allow it to, and now Pastor Shoemaker is headed down that road.

It's September 8th and Pastor Shoemaker is in the pulpit doing what God has called him to do. The Miracle and Deliverance service is going on. The congregation has been wondering where First Lady Shoemaker is and also pastor's right hand man, Brother Carl. They also notice that the service is dry and there aren't any miracles taking place or any deliverances occurring. They sense and see that their pastor appears to be weak and no longer confident. "Something is wrong." each man and woman said in their hearts.

Pastor Shoemaker felt guilty, condemned, hurt, confused and full of fear. Yes, what Pastor Shoemaker has done is wrong. Yes, he needs help. However, the only one that can help him is God. Pastor Shoemaker has been running from God. He needs to be running to God. Can you see what sin does? It makes you into a coward!

Pastor Shoemaker no longer has confidence in God to use him to cause miracles and deliverance in the lives of people. He does not understand that he is the righteousness of God. What does the righteousness of God mean? It means being in right standing with God, without any sense of guilt, condemnation or inferiority, as though sin had never existed. All Pastor Shoemaker has to do is stand in the presence of God with confidence and say, "Lord, I missed the mark. I made a mistake and according to 1 John 1:9, you said that if I'd confess my sin with my mouth that you'd be faithful and just to forgive me of my sins and cleanse me from all unrighteousness." Then he could thank and praise God that He has forgiven him and move on to answer God's call.

Now he has confidence in God. Now anyone he lays hands on will be healed and delivered. However, when you don't understand the righteousness of God or your rights, you now don't have confidence in God that he can do anything for you in any arena of life. At that point, you have turned off the power because, like Pastor Shoemaker, you dwell in the puddle of sin. Instead, you should be waking up the superhero in you, cleaning yourself off and shouting, "It does not matter what I have done or what I did last night, last week, last month, last year or ten years ago! God has forgiven me and has cleansed me from that sin and has caused me to change so that he can give me more super powers for the next level in my life."

Can you see now that this is all Pastor Shoemaker had to do—awake to his righteousness and sin not! Once he did that he'd begin to see miracles and deliverances explode in his church more than ever before. Well, you may ask, what about his wife and kids? God specializes in fixing situations like this as long as Pastor Shoemaker continues to make changes and keeps taking care of God's business first. It does not matter how tragic it may be or how impossible it may seem, you and God will get the last laugh of victory.

You may be a pastor who has experienced the same situation. You may be in another job and have done some awful, off the chain things in your life. You, man of God, may be stuck in a situation right now and may not know how to get out. You may have been putting up with things in your life that have been tearing you down! Well that's over for you. How? Because as you continue to read you are about to learn your rights with God so that you can stand in the presence of a Almighty God and become a super righteous hero instead of a super failure. Let's read on!

# Super Section Two: Understanding your position as the righteousness of God

The Bible says in Proverbs 4:7,

*In all your getting, get understanding.*

Most men don't understand their righteous stance with God. They don't have a clue about the rights that have been given to them by God. I'm talking about men from every faith: Baptist, Pentecostal, Catholic, Muslim, Jehovah Witness, Christian, Word of Faith, or even the guy who has not been born again. It does not matter what title of religion you carry around or if you go to church a hundred times a week and do good deeds. What truly matters is your own personal relationship with God, understanding your righteous position and your rights with God. An umpire in baseball understands his stance as he stands behind the shoulder of the catcher looking to see if the baseball that the pitcher throws is valid or not. The umpire understands his rights in calling a certain pitch. He has the right to call a certain pitch a strike or not. It's all up to him. He calls and controls that portion of the game. Why? He has a right to. Well, on that note, we as men are playing the game of life, but far too many of us are striking out when it's time to step up to the plate. There are some special baseball players who have the power to knock a baseball out of the park. But what's the difference between the baseball player who can't knock baseballs out of the park and the one who can? The baseball player who hits baseballs out of the park understands that he has a right to have an opportunity to hit a baseball and demonstrate his power that he worked hard for in knocking baseballs out of the park. The baseball player who does not knock baseballs out of the park does not understand that he has a right too. You may say, "Well, not every baseball player can hit a baseball out of the park!" Oh, yes they can! How? By using their right to go out and work hard, developing their baseball skills just like the other baseball player did. Did you know that every man on the planet could be a millionaire, including you? "Yeah, right, everybody isn't going to be a millionaire." Do you know why? Because they'll never understand that they have a right to become one. They'll never use their right to think and use their right to ask God for wisdom to make them a millionaire so that they can be a blessing on the earth.

Most men today are being controlled by Satan and his demons, including the churchgoing man who professes to be a Christian. It's sad but true. How do I know? Because I used to be one of them, and I know some of them. Men are angry, full of fear, lust, pride, selfishness; they are broke, sick, diseased, dis-eased, stressed and lonely. They divorce their wives because of lust as well as hateful, malicious and unforgiving attitudes. They're addicted to drugs, alcohol and sex. Some are racist, lazy and lack vision. They have no goals in sight. They practice witchcraft, indulge in pornography. They're insecure, depressed, workaholics who fear failure. They have got low self-esteem, no hope and aren't able to give or receive love. They aren't willing to take care of their kids. If you have found yourself showing or having one or more of these demonic traits, you simply don't realize who you are as the righteousness of God. Did you know the moment you gave your life to God through his son Jesus Christ, you became the righteousness of God? In Romans 5:17 it states that,

*For if by the one man's offense death reigned (ruled) through the one, much more those who receive abundance of grace and of the gift of righteousness will reign (rule) in life through the one , Jesus Christ.*

God's number one creation as far as human beings was Adam. God intended for Adam to rule and reign throughout the whole earth. Bu that first man, Adam, messed up God's entire plan for man. Adam was deceived and enticed with the fruit that was given to him. This incident is known as "the fall of man." However, I have a question for you. Why are men still falling, even as Christians? Man of God, one of the reasons why is because mankind was born into sin. The second we came out of our mother's womb we were born into sin. We didn't have to purchase sin with our credit cards; we were just made sinners based on Adam's offense. But after the fall of man, God had another plan–to send his only begotten son, Jesus Christ, to save us from that sinful nature. Jesus, when he was beaten and mistreated, took up all of our infirmities, sickness and disease, poverty, Satan's evil bondages, and everything else that represented sin. He took it all to the cross and died for you and me. Why? So that we could receive a free gift from God the minute we got born again not by coming back out of a womb of a woman, but by confessing and believing that Jesus Christ was raised from the dead and that he is Lord over your life. Not only did you receive Jesus, you then became or were made in the righteousness of God. You are no longer made in sin, once you have received Jesus and his grace. Jesus is also known as the second Adam. He passed the test that Adam failed. Although Satan tempted Jesus, Jesus never failed! Jesus knew who he was, the righteousness of God! This is why he was able to rule and reign throughout the earth.

This is why, through Jesus Christ as Lord and Savior of your life, you have the ability to rule and reign like a king in your life. This is the very reason why God wants you to find out who you really are so that you can start doing what he first intended mankind to do: be fruitful, multiply, rule and reign over Satan and this dark world.

You may say, "How could I say I'm the righteousness of God? Why I am still struggling with this and that? How can I rule and reign on the earth when I have committed this sin so many times?" First of all, will you please stop allowing the enemy to whisper those thoughts to you? Next, get rid of the good and the bad checklist that you seem to be keeping. Always remember and meditate on the fact that the righteousness of God was a free gift. It's a powerful force you can use at any time. Remember also that the righteousness of God is the ability to stand in the presence of God without a sense of guilt, condemnation or inferiority–as though sin never existed. You cannot do more good deeds such as attending church more, striving to be better and do more than the rest of the ushers at the church. This type of living will always cause you to work for righteousness instead of receiving your free gift of righteousness and accepting the fact that you were made that way.

So what happens when I sin? Good question! And here's another question by way of answer. What happens when you slip and fall down on the ground and get dirty? It's simple–you just get up and dust yourself off and move on. Likewise, when you commit a sin, don't allow the devil to speak negative words to you such as, "Ha, ha. See there, I knew you weren't delivered from that! Look at you! You are supposed to be a Christian! How can you lift your hands and praise God! You are a fake Christian!" Such negativity will cause you to run from God instead of running to him. When you sin just, use your righteousness to get out. You already have been given the right to stand before God without any guilt or inferiority and simply ask God to forgive you of whatever it was you did.

Most people take this right and abuse it! How? By saying, "I can do this or do that. God will forgive me because he promised that." But remember, every sin has a price tag attached, labeled "consequences"!!! Why would you play Russian roulette with your life by sinning? For example, why grieve the Holy Spirit, your helper, by having sex with someone before marriage and end up with a baby out of wedlock, or perhaps catch some kind of disease such as AIDS, syphilis, gonorrhea, etc. Do not allow Satan to trick you by saying, "Go ahead. No one will know. It's okay, just one more time. Go ahead and do your brother or sister in Christ wrong, they did you wrong." When the pleasure is all over, Satan will forget to show you the other side of the coin, which shows death not only physically but spiritually as well. You are a man of God who does not practice sin. You are striving on a daily basis to find a way out of sin. Practiced sin will only cause a separation between you and God.

I can recall when I struggled with masturbation. It was a serious addiction. I battled with not stopping and wanting to stop. Sometimes I enjoyed it and other times I didn't. Why? Because I was so sin conscious. Whenever I masturbated or committed some other sin I immediately ran from God instead of coming to the throne of grace and mercy and asking him for help! That was and still is our right! How? Because his word says in Hebrews 4:16,

*Let us therefore come boldly to the throne of grace, that we may obtain mercy and find grace to help in the time of need.*

God is willing and wanting to help you right now as you are reading this book. You are a child of God; get that in your thinking! Look at John 1:12 which reads,

*But as many as received him, to them he gave the right to become children of God to those who believe in his name.*

Did you just see that! You have been given the right to become a child of God. Why? You have received his son, Jesus Christ, as Lord over your life. God is your heavenly father! You ought to meditate on the fact that God is your father. For those of you who didn't have an opportunity to have a relationship with your father, you no longer have to feel rejected. So end all the excuses such as "I didn't have a father so I can't do this" or "I don't know how to do that." I once had the same excuses. Not having a loving, caring, and supporting father around was tormenting, especially when I looked up into the stands and saw other guys' fathers there instead of my own at my football games and track meets. I know how important a father's role is in a child's life. If you have kids, whether boys or girls, their daddy is the foundation of their life. Encourage your children to be the best that they can be. You'll see how effective you were when they come back and tell you after they have grown up, "Thank you, dad, for being there for me."

After I began to meditate on the fact that God is my heavenly father, I began to change my view on not having a father in my life. I do have a father and he really, truly loves me and is concerned about my wellbeing. He is a father who is always there for me. He is always in me and with me. The earth is his and the fullness that's in it! He owns just about everything that you see, and he always comes to my aid when I call upon him. What kind of father would God be if he never answered when you called? He'd be worthless. You can be glad that He's not like that, Amen. However, some of you act like you think this way. Why? You won't use the right that you have with God. He told you whenever you get into trouble or need some help to come boldly to the throne of grace where he is located and ask for help.

So, the big question is, "Why don't men take advantage of this one right?" It's all because of sin consciousness instead of righteousness consciousness. Men of God truly don't want to sin and don't have to. Don't allow sin to rule over you. Instead, you rule over it how by using your super power, your righteousness! Look with me at Romans 6:12-16,

*Therefore, don't let sin reign (rule) in your mortal body, that you should obey it in its lusts. And don't present your members as instruments of unrighteousness to sin, but present yourselves to God as being alive from the dead, and your members as instruments of righteousness to God. For sin shall not have dominion over you. For you are not under law but under grace. What then? Shall we sin because we are not under law but under grace? Certainly not! Do you not know that to whom you present yourselves slaves to obey, you are that one's slave whom you obey, whether of sin leading to death, or of obedience leading to righteousness?*

You were created to win and to dominate over any sinful act that you are struggling with. As you see in verse 15, you are no longer under the law but you are under and protected by grace. Does that give you a permit to sin? Of course not! The Bible says, "Don't frustrate the grace of God." You are no longer a slave to sin! I speak my faith over you right now, as you are reading this book.
Your present-day obedience determines your future harvest. If you haven't made a decision to obey God's Word by stepping off the foundation of sin and standing firm on the foundation of your righteousness, please do so. If not, you could be holding up your harvest that you believe God for, which is a wealth of superhero power of "righteousness." Look with me at II Timothy 2:21-22, which states,

*Therefore, if anyone cleanses himself from the latter, he'll be a vessel for honor, sanctified and useful for the Master, prepared for every good work. Flee also youthful lusts: but pursue righteousness, faith, love, peace with those who call on the Lord out of a pure heart.*

Man of God, begin evaluating your lifestyle. Ask yourself, "What am I doing that's not absolutely pleasing to God? Could this be the reason why I can't hear from God?" If your spirit is cluttered all up with a practiced sin, be honest with yourself and pursue your power of righteousness. You may ask, "How do I do that? It's hard to stop doing what I'm doing. I want to stop but my brakes are not working." Read with me in Ephesians 5:26,

*That he might sanctify and cleanse her with the washing of water by the word.*

In order to clean out a dirty sink, you may need a can of Ajax, some scrubbing sponges, and a pair of rubber gloves. You could have all of these products, but not do a good job. Why? Because you don't have water! However, once you add water to the cleaning products, you can get rid of the dirt in the sink, and the sink is now available for use.

You probably have been using the world's products such as worldly counseling, the psychic's line, other people's advice (though they're hurting too), anger management groups, rehabilitation centers, etc. Some of these products are good. However, good without God is bad! A more powerful substance will clean just about anything that is dirty, and that is the word of God. In the scripture you just read, it says that the word will wash out all the dirt of sin that's built upon your heart and mind. Look for scriptures pertaining to the righteousness of God and scrub out your heart and mind with the word of God. Begin to look in the word, locate your rights, and meditate on them. Look for scriptures about these rights:

- The right to know who you really are.
- The right to come to God boldly when you need help.
- The right to rule and reign on this earth like a king.
- The right to get wisdom and understanding from God.
- The right to healing in and on your physical body.
- The right to sow a seed and receive a harvest.
- The right to be wealthy, rich and prosperous.
- The right to be victorious and overcome any obstacle in this world.
- The right to answered prayer.
- The right to be just like Jesus.
- The right to be just like God.
- The right to the Holy Spirit.
- The right to win, period, in life.

You are the righteousness of God! I am sure that you have gained a better understanding of who you really are in Christ. But there's one more important thing. Knowing that you have rights isn't good enough, just like having a car without a motor isn't good enough. Knowing that you have rights with God as the righteousness of God will be ineffective if you are not ready to operate in those rights. However, Christians try to use these rights just to end up disappointed. Now does the disappointment occur because God's word only works sometimes? Of course not! Someone may say, "I tried that righteousness stuff and it doesn't work for me!" No, I believe it's the other way around, righteousness tried you! No part of God's word ever fails. There was a reason why it didn't work for you. And that's what we're getting ready to look at.

## Super Section Three: Condemnation will kill confidence in your righteousness

*For the law of the spirit of life in Christ Jesus has made me*
*Free from the law of sin and death. (Romans 8:2)*

When a man operates or turns on the law of sin and death, it will ultimately destroy his confidence in God. As you'll read throughout this book, confidence is the substance that will turn on the law of the spirit of life in Christ Jesus and bring you complete freedom so that you can become the man that God intended for you to be. Condemnation is when a man feels bad about himself for committing sin. He thinks that God is mad at him and no longer wants to use him or bless him. I am one of those men who used to think this way. Every time I committed a sin or missed the mark, I'd say, "That's it! God is mad at me. He isn't going to answer my prayers. He isn't going to give me the desires of my heart. He definitely isn't going to prosper me. I may as well stop confessing his word because the God and the angels aren't listening. When I am in trouble there is no need to call on God because he won't help me anyway, since I have been sinning."

Does this sound like you when you mess up and sin? If so, this could be the main reason why the free gift of the righteousness of God hasn't kicked in yet in your life. Sin will make you a coward when your righteousness will make you a man full of confidence in God. I had to decide one day to believe the word of God concerning condemnation. There was no what if, maybe, etc. I just made up my mind and believed in Romans 8:1,

*There is therefore now no condemnation to those who are in Christ Jesus.*

This means that when I sin or miss the mark I don't have to condemn myself. I have a choice to make: either continue to feel sorry for myself and have no confidence in God, or receive the free gift of righteousness that says no matter what sin you have committed you have a right to go and ask God for forgiveness. He takes that sin, throws it into the sea of forgetfulness, and remembers it no more. So if that's the case, why would I want to remember that sin I committed when God has given me the right to remember it no more?

God is simple. Why do we make things so hard for ourselves when we mess up! I used to ask myself that. I know that you may have asked yourself the same thing. Well, just know that God made you righteous.

Also keep this very important point near and dear to your heart:

that Jesus has already paid the price for every sin that you have committed or will commit. If you miss it, big deal! Get up and keep moving forward, just don't allow sin. Why? Because when sin is fully grown, it will cause death. Superheroes get up when they fall down. They don't condemn themselves. They're like Jesus! They die to sin and resurrect themselves with the help of God and continue to pursue a life of victory having no condemnation, but having all confidence in their righteous stance in God. You are the righteousness of God! Take authority of this power you have. After all, that's what superheroes do– take authority!!!

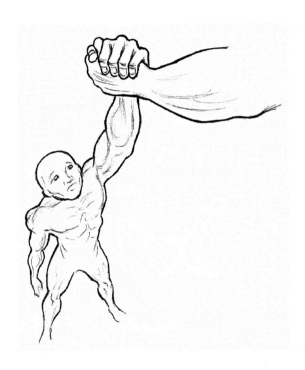

# Chapter Five

## Super Section One: A Marked Minded Man cannot be stopped!

*He'll be ever mindful of his covenant. (Psalm 110:5)*

Have you ever wondered what would really happen if God answered every prayer as soon as you prayed or even showed up in any situation when you called him? Have you ever really thought about what it would be like to have a relationship and be used by God like Moses, David, Solomon, and Jesus himself?

What if I told you that you no longer have to wonder if God would answer your prayers? As soon as you pray them, God does really desire to be in relationship with you and use you to work for Him. Well, it's true–this can really happen for you! You may say, "I don't believe you because I tried that Christian faith stuff and it didn't work for me!" First and foremost, you don't have to believe me, but instead believe the words that are coming from your Bible. Secondly, I must ask as I did in Chapter Three, "Did you really with all of your heart try faith or did faith try you?" Men tend to always give up and quit in anything in life when what they believed in wasn't rooted and grounded in their heart. You can get God Almighty to move on your behalf in any arena of your life including your present situation and circumstances. It does not matter how big, how impossible the problems that you are facing today may be, God is ready to shoot to your aid just as fast as a bullet speeds from a shot gun!

Yes, you may have wondered over and over again, "How come as a man of God I'm not fully receiving the promises of God in my life? Why can I not get God to show up in my life when the battles of life are overwhelming and experience God's victorious power like the prophets of old experienced?" We both know it's not God's fault. He's perfect and all knowing. Once again, men, anything that is unsuccessful or didn't work, there was a cause for whatever it was. Now, men of God, please understand the fact that when you don't know who you really are in Christ, many causes of failure come from that alone.

This brings me to this chapter's topic–The Covenant– another super power that has been sleeping soundly within you. Having your mind marked with a covenant from God will cause you to operate like a superhero such as Abraham, Joseph, David and Jesus. These men knew that they had a covenant with God and as they continued to do what God asked them to do, God continued to do whatever they had asked him to do for them, which made them look like superheroes in the eyes of others. And that is what exactly God wants the people at your job, in your family, in your church, in your community, in your relationships, in the entire universe to see, the superhero that God created you to be.

What is a covenant? A covenant is a pledge, promise, vow, or agreement between two or more parties. A covenant isn't a contract because a contract can be broken. The only way that a covenant can be broken is by death! God takes the covenant he makes with men seriously. In today's world, we make many promises, agreements, and vows and then break them thoughtlessly. Consider marriage vows–did you know Christians are having more divorces than marriages outside Christianity? Why? Because Christians don't take the marriage covenant seriously. They either don't understand the vow's importance or they (men and women) go after their own selfish, lustful desires. If children are involved, they get hurt and grow up practicing divorce in their relationships even when they get married.

Now that you understand that a covenant is an agreement, vow, promise or pledge that you can make with God that can only be broken by death, let's look a little deeper at this covenant. Many men are strangers to this covenant–agreement, vow, promise, or pledge–that they have with God. Look with me at Ephesians 2:11-12,

> *Therefore, remember that you, once Gentiles in the flesh–who are called uncircumcision by what is called the circumcision made in the flesh by hands– that at the time you were without Christ, being aliens from the commonwealth of Israel and strangers from the covenants of promise, having no hope and without God in the world.*

How can you tell if a man does not know who he really is in Christ? When he walks around saying that he is a Christian but you cannot see any evidence of God's promises in his life and he lives without hope. You mean to tell me that he could be a Christian and go to church and shout hallelujah a thousand times? Absolutely! It does not matter if you are a sinner or a Christian. If you don't understand the power that lies within you, the power of knowing your covenant with God, you could very well be living out the scripture in Ephesians 2, having no hope in the world.

This could explain why success has not visited your life, because you have found out that you have been a victim of being a stranger to your covenant–your agreement, promise, vow, or pledge with God.

Being a stranger to your covenant is being like Jesse, who always wanted to go to college and pursue a degree in medicine. He was extremely smart and graduated at the top of his class. He also had a passion to put formulas together to help cure diseases. This is why he desired to go into the medical field.

Jesse and his mom lived together in a very small two-bedroom apartment. Growing up without a father was very difficult for 18-year-old Jesse. He was always looking for that father figure in his life and never had a chance to obtain it. Some of you grew up without a father and wanted him to be around. However, he wasn't there for whatever reason. This can be painful. I know—I've felt that pain! However, it can get better. How? By believing and receiving God as your father, because he and only he can fill that void. Spend time with him and you'll see.

Jesse's father, who was mentally retarded, died when he was three years old, from leukemia. However, Jesse's paternal grandfather just passed away a year ago. Jesse's grandfather always knew Jesse's father couldn't provide for him. Now, Jesse's grandfather stayed in contact with him by mail because he was on the West Coast and Jessie and his mom were on the East Coast. However, every time Jesse's mom checked the mailbox and saw a letter from Jesse's grandfather, she'd tear the letter up. Why? She was still angry over a matter that took place when she and Jesse's father were together. After Jesse's mom learned his grandfather passed away, she opened a letter Jesse's grandfather sent him two months before he died. The reason why Jesse's mom didn't tear this particular letter was because of the words that were written across the back of the envelope: "Whatever my son did to you, please forgive him, I really miss my grandson." After she heard that Jesse's grandfather had died, she called Jesse into the kitchen and told him to have a seat.

"I want you to read a letter that your grandfather had sent you before he died."

Jesse slowly took the letter, puzzled by the thought, "I really don't know my grandfather!" He unfolded the letter and it read:

*Dear Jesse,*

*I've been writing you but I haven't gotten a response yet. I have asked your mom to forgive your father for what happened between them. I guess your mom will tell you all that went down before your father died.*

*I always wanted you to spend some time with me, so we could get to know each other. The doctors say I don't have much time left because of this tumor on my brain. In case I don't hear from you before I die, I just want to know I love and miss you. Hopefully, we'll meet again in heaven. I also left you a gift from my heart and your father's. I left you $100,000. Give your Aunt Lucille and my lawyer a call, so you can get your inheritance. It's your money. Spend it wisely. Buy a house or go to college. Make the right choices. Trust in God and keep him in first place always.*

*P.S. (Lawyer) Melvin Cox * 1-555-633-666*
   *Aunt Lucille Washington * 1-555-336-7777*

*Love Grandpa*

Now, as Jesse was reading the letter, his mother began crying and shaking her head. She knew she was wrong for keeping her son away from his grandfather. Jesse began crying too and asked his mom, "Why?" She explained and apologized, he forgave her, and they hugged. The previous year, Jesse had wanted to attend college but he couldn't. Why? No money! He then looked into his mother's eyes and said, "Mom! I can now go to college."

The point that I want you to see is that Jesse was a stranger to his inheritance, because his mom had hidden the letters from him for a long time. She also didn't know that there was a $100,000 inheritance just waiting for him. That's how sinners and many Christians are living. Are you, man of God, a stranger to your covenant with God? God has so much inheritance waiting just for you. It is time for you to discover another part of who you are! You are a covenant man with God and God has a mighty harvest just for you. If you'll continue to read, you'll realize that you are no longer a stranger to your covenant.

The desire of my heart is to help you develop a covenant consciousness: a covenant attitude towards God, and the pledge, agreement, vow, and promise that will be branded on your mind so that you can live a life like God who is always mindful of his covenant with you.

# Super Section Two: God is always looking for a man to make a covenant with

God is always looking for a man that he can mark. In other words, he's looking to make an agreement, promise, pledge, or vow with a man who has a strong desire to serve him with all of his heart. In today's society, numerous men are marked by "America's Most Wanted." The FBI has marked men that they're watching and looking for. Saddam Hussein was a marked man until the United States Armed Forces captured him. Bin Laden is still a marked man throughout the world. Once I was put on probation for a couple of years by the judicial system. I became a marked man.

In a negative case, it does not feel good to be a marked man. I don't know how or where your life is concerning how people view you. Are you marked on your job as a good worker or a bad worker? Are you a husband marked as loving, caring, and sharing, or are you marked by your children and wife as a mean, hateful, and selfish husband and father? In your professional career or as a business owner, are you marked as someone with honesty, integrity, and good work ethic, or are you marked as someone who cheats, manipulates, and exhibits a slothful and lazy attitude. Perhaps you're a minister. What is your ministry marked by: excellence and loving people, or by half-heartedness and pressuring money out of people? Did you know your children are a reflection of you and people will mark your children based on the training that you gave them? In the Bible days, God even marked men, those he used, according to his purpose. Look with me at Genesis 4:15,

*And the Lord said to him, "Therefore, whoever kills Cain, vengeance shall be taken on him sevenfold." And the Lord set a mark on Cain, lest anyone finding him should kill him.*

After Cain had killed his brother Abel for giving God a offering from his heart which God had accepted while he rejected Cain's offering, God spoke to Cain and told him that as long as he was on this earth he'd be a fugitive. Therefore, Cain responded by saying, "My punishment is too great. How can I live a life of peace when you have just announced that I'll become a fugitive and whoever finds me will kill me?" But God never said that someone was going to kill him; he only said that Cain would be a fugitive. And in verse 15, as you already have read, God gave Cain comfort by putting a mark or a covenant–promise, pledge, agreement, or vow–of protection over his life. Now Cain knows that God will protect him. He can live his life with security and in confidence that God is with him.

I'm not exactly sure what that mark was but I can only guess that is was the presence of God upon him and when enemies tried to come up against Cain to kill him, they couldn't do it! Why? They recognized the mark that was on his life.

There's something about a man who stays in the presence of God. That man cannot be stopped! He's the guy who always comes out on top like the superhero that he is. His power comes from opening up his Bible and finding out what God has said about him. He does not only read what it says about him but he acts on what God said about him while he was in the presence of God. His mind has been marked with the covenants of God. The man I'm talking about is you.

Now let's take a moment and find out where this covenant started. Who exactly did God first cut covenant with? Did the covenant work with the first man? Would this guy that God first made covenant with be a good example for us to follow? If he was a covenant man, what kind of super powers did he possess? Look with me at Genesis 15:1-8,

*After these things the word of the Lord came to Abram in a vision, saying, "Don't be afraid, Abram. I am your shield, your exceedingly great reward." But Abram said, "Lord God, what will you give me,*

*seeing I go childless, and the heir of my house is Eliezer of Damascus?"*
*Then Abram said, "Look, you have given me no offspring: indeed one*
*born in my house is my heir!" And behold, the word of the Lord came*
*to him saying, "This one shall not be your heir, but one who will come*
*from your own body shall be your heir!" Then he brought him outside*
*and said, "Look toward heaven, and count the stars if you are able*
*to number them." And he said, "So shall your seed be." And he believed*
*in the Lord, and he counted it to him for righteousness. The he said to*
*him, "I am the Lord, who brought you out of Ur of the Chaldeans, to*
*give you this land to inherit it. And he said, "Lord God, how shall I know*
*that I'll inherit it?"*

As you can clearly see, God found himself a man that he could make a covenant with. The man's name was Abram. Before God had showed up to cut covenant with Abram, he was found worshipping the moon. Abram had no idea, while he was worshipping the moon, that he was praising what God himself created. In every man's life, there is a desire to worship something. God has created a place in every man's heart where he only belongs. Nothing else belongs there. However, we men have tried to replace God with other things and people such as cars, money, women, wife, children, careers, recreation, etc.

I remember I was in the same situation as Abram was once in. Instead of worshipping the moon, I found myself worshipping the females I was in relationship with or worshipping the sport of football, training every day to become a professional football player. My goal was to please the woman I was with instead of pleasing God first! My dream was to become a professional football player instead of focusing in on God's dream and that's to bring people to Jesus Christ. Neither one worked out while I worshipped them both. Neither did Abram get any of his prayers answered or receive healing when he was worshipping the moon.

Do you understand why nothing worked in our lives? Abram's and my priorities were wrong. God wasn't number one. But the things we worshipped were. Ask yourself this question, what do I find myself worshipping the most in my life other than God? Could that be why I'm experiencing a drought? If you have honestly answered these questions, it's okay if your answer made you feel unworthy. There is always good news. Notice how God still chose Abram to make a covenant with, although he was worshipping the moon. God didn't say, " I can't use him to make a covenant with; he's a moon worshiper." No! Instead, he said, "Yes! I finally found a man that I can make a covenant with! Although he's worshipping the moon, I can use his same zeal that he uses to worship the moon with and turn his heart to worship me if he chooses to. And I'll prosper his life because of his obedience towards me, something the moon couldn't do!"

What a perfect candidate to make a covenant with. There is

absolutely nothing wrong with having a car or cars, a good career, a lot of money, a soul mate or things you like in general. The problem comes in when you have a wrong relationship with those things. God wants men to seek his face so that he can give them what's in his hands. Learn to put first things first as God begins to speak with you in the rest of this chapter.

God then showed himself to Abram in a vision and told him that he was going to have a son. God even told Abram to go outside and look at the sky and asked him if he could number all of the stars in the sky. God said that's how many children would come from his one and only son. In verse six, Abram believed God and that was counted as righteousness. Not only that, God turns right around and promises Abram that he was going to give him some land to inherit. Isn't interesting, after God made Abram a promise he questions God in verse eight and says to God, "Lord God, how shall I know that I'll inherit it. (meaning the land and promised child)."

We as men often do the same thing. We look into God's word and he promises that he's going to give us an abundant life, the desires of our heart, wealth, healing, restoration, deliverance, and whatever else that you could believe God for. We ask God the same questions: God, how do I know that you are going to meet all my needs and my family needs? God, how do I know that you are going to really deliver me from this addiction? God, how do I know you'll help my business or ministry grow? God, how do I know you're going to help make my dreams come true? God, how do I know that you'll never leave me nor forsake me?

Does that honestly sound like you? I know, at one time, when I didn't fully trust God, I asked that question often. Until I read in verse 18 God answering Abram's question:

*On the same day, the Lord made a covenant.*

In other words, he said to Abram, "In order for you to believe in me and know for a surety that I'll do this, I'm going to make a pledge to you."

I'd like to pause right there and give you a clear example of what's going on. When I'm talking about this subject, I often tell people about the Williams and Burg families. The Williams lived in an old project complex near downtown in the big city. The Williams family consists of Otis Williams, his wife, Etta, and five sons: Otis Jr., Oliver, Robert, James and Stanley, who range in age from 18 to 25 years old. These guys were the toughest in the neighborhood. They were street smart and knew how to protect themselves. They lived in a tough environment. Bedroom windows were cracked. There wasn't any glass in the kitchen windows. The toilet and sinks barely worked. In the summer, the two-bedroom housing project was terribly hot! There wasn't any air conditioning. In the winter, it was extremely cold because there wasn't any heat. The Williams family had just enough clothing to get by. Their clothes were very, very old—shirts with holes, and shoes begin to expand even more. You may be thinking why the dad and those five boys of his wouldn't just go to work! It's a shame to say but it's the same reason why the majority of men won't work, because of laziness! They'd all try to get themselves jobs but their appearance was always a problem. (That's no excuse! Look neat by getting a haircut, brush your teeth and wash your mouth out with Listerine, wear freshly ironed clothing. Always wear a necktie—it will indicate that you mean business.)

No character, no morals, but yet a tough family. They lived off unemployment checks and government food. This was a very poor family with no purpose in life. They had no direction. They only knew the street life. They got what they could get free from the government and lived off their reputation of being the toughest in the neighborhood.

Just about thirty minutes out of the downtown area was the Burg family, who lived in a nice suburban subdivision. The Burg family consists of the father, Mr. Burg, his wife and his two daughters. Mr. Burg was a business owner of a Fortune Five Hundred company. When you see Mr. Burg or hear Mr. Burg's name, you think of one word: "millionaire"! He was a very successful businessman, and he was a very successful husband to his wife plus a successful father to his children. Mr. Burg knew everything about being a man of purpose, character, and right moral living.

But there was one problem that kept occurring in the Burg household. Every time Mr. Burg traveled, burglars broke into the Burg estate. The big gated and alarmed fence was no threat to the burglars. Mr. Burg knew he had to do something about the invasions of his home. He knew that he had to find some protection for his family and he found a solution. Mr. Burg had heard about the viciousness and toughness of the Williams family. After he and his wife had a discussion on what it was going to take to protect the family, they both agreed to form their own security company. (Please stop listing to the false statement that having a lot of money is bad. It's not bad when it's in the right hands. You can do many awesome things with money. Just think about it—what can you do broke?) So Mr. Burg drove to the projects near downtown to find the toughest guys in the city. After asking several people where he could find the Williams family, he finally discovered where they lived. Like a soldier on a mission, he went up to the door and knocked. Mr. Burg saw the doorbell didn't work and it smelled. Trash was all over the yard. Finally, the six foot nine inch father answered the door and said harshly, "Yes! Can I help you?" and "Who are you?"

Mr. Burg began to stutter, looking up at Mr. Williams as though he was Mt. Zion, and said, "Hi...my, my, my name, na...name...is Mr., Mr.,...Mr. Burg!"

Mr. Williams said to him, "What's wrong? Are you scared or

something?"

Mr. Burg answered by saying, "Yes, sir! I mean no, sir!" He *was* frightened because he'd never seen anyone so tall and big.

Mr. Williams then said to him, "What are you doing in a neighborhood like this one? You'd better make sure that the doors are locked and the alarm on that pearl white Mercedes-Benz is on."

"Yes, sir!" Mr. Burg answered, "I have already taken care of that. The reason for my coming over was to ask you for a favor."

Mr. Williams retorted, "Ask me for a favor! I can't even invite you into my home because we don't have any furniture and we haven't vacuumed the carpet in three weeks because the vacuum broke, unless you want to sit on the carpet Indian style with the rest of the family."

"No, sir, I think I...I'll pass on that one." Mr. Burg no longer was frightened because he kept the thought in his mind, "I've got to protect my family". So he looked Mr. Williams in the eye, stood toe to toe with him and said, "I am here to see if you can help me and I am definitely here to help you!"

After Mr. Williams saw and heard the boldness from Mr. Burg, he then said, "Okay, Mr. Burg, how can I help you?"

Mr. Burg explained, "I live in the suburbs, about thirty minutes from here. I have a very large, gated estate. But it's left unattended whenever I go out of town on a business trip. Not only that, I have a beautiful wife and two girls and I really have to protect them."

Mr. Williams said, "I understand that but how can I help you?"

Mr. Burg replied, "I heard about you and your boys. They say they're the toughest in the city!"

"That's absolutely true about my boys and we've had our share of victories with their problems they try to come against!" Mr. Williams said confidently.

"I also recognize your living conditions are very poor," Mr. Burg said, "so here's what I am willing to do, if you and your boys will come out to my place to protect my estate. I'll build you and your family a new house, I'll put everyone on my payroll, I'll always load your home with groceries and I'll purchase you and your wife a vehicle of your choice. Also, I'll buy each of your five boys a brand new car. But that's if you'll only protect my family and my estate."

Mr. Williams asked, "You mean to tell me all that I have to do is send myself and my boys to your home and protect it and you'll do all that?"

"That's correct, Mr. Williams."

Mr. Williams immediately agreed, "Okay in exchange for what you said you'd do, we'll make sure your family will be protected and secured and do our very best by giving you 100% protective services because we know that we cannot be stopped."

Mr. Burg and Mr. Williams shook hands and put things in writing, and they became the "Williamsburg" family. Now, Mr. Burg had another business: His own security services firm. Mr. Williams and his family now had meaning and a purpose in life. Both families have made exchanges for strengths and weaknesses. Both families have made a covenant with each other–a promise, pledge, agreement, or vow between two or more parties. As long as Mr. Burg continues to do his part of the covenant, it will never be broken and as long as Mr. Williams continues to do his part by protecting the Burg family, the Williamsburg family covenant will never be broken.

This is a perfect example of what took place between God and Abram. God promised Abram a son and some land. That was God's part, but what was Abram's part of the covenant? Look with me at Genesis 17:9-12,

*And God said to Abraham, "As for you, you shall keep my covenant, you and your descendants after you throughout their generations. This is my covenant which you shall keep, between me and you and your descendants after you: every male child among you shall be circumcised in the flesh of your foreskins, and it shall be a sign of the covenant between me and you. He who is eight days old among you shall be circumcised, every male child in your generations.*

Before we go on, did you notice in the beginning of verse nine, it says, "And God said to Abraham"? His name is no longer Abram, but Abraham. So why did God change his name? As you are still in Chapter 17, go up to verse five which states,

*No longer shall your name be called Abram, but your name shall be Abraham; for I have made you a father of many nations.*

God had changed Abraham's name because his new name had purpose behind it! His name had meaning behind it! There were people who probably came up to Abraham and asked him his name. And Abraham would confidently say, "My name is Abraham–a father of many nations!" When you think of the name of Clark Kent who do you think of? "Superman." When you think of the name Bruce Wayne, who do you think of? "Batman." In 2007, when you think of the name of the president, who do you think of? "George W. Bush." When you hear the name of Pastor Creflo A. Dollar, Jr., what do you think of? "Prosperity." When you hear the name of Jesus Christ what do you immediately think of? My savior, my healer, my protector, my brother, and my friend. If you could use one word for all of the above names what would it be? I'd use the name of a force that always gets results and the name is "power." Each name that was mentioned represents power.

So what is your name? Many men don't know what their names mean. Why? You don't know who you are. Jacob's name meant trickster, and then God changed it to Israel. Simon was a fisherman, and Jesus changed his name to Peter, "the rock." Your name represents you. You may say, I don't know what my name means. As you begin to find out who you really are in Christ, you'll locate a new meaning to your name and you'll begin to realize the power behind your name. Your name is no longer the loser, the ex-convict, the dope drug dealer, the rapist, the murderer, the jealous and insecure one, the one who will never be anything in life. Instead, your name is Son of God, a mighty man of valor, a god on this planet (notice small g), and a man who God always allows to be victorious. You'll find your name as you begin to find yourself.

As you can see in verse 12, Abraham's part was to take every 8-day-old male child and have them circumcised on the foreskin of their penis. This was a mark God wanted on every male in the house of Abraham and around Abraham. The mark of circumcision was a permanent sign showing that a person was in covenant with God. It wasn't stopping those that were under the protection of God. Abraham kept his side of the covenant. He was extremely obedient towards God! Back in Abraham's day, they sacrificed animals and walked in their blood. They also used to cut their hands and rub them together as they made a blood covenant. This is why when God made covenant with Abraham; he had to get on Abraham's level of thinking so this thing could make sense to him. He instructed Abraham to go out and get certain animals. Look at Genesis 15:9-10,

*So he said to him, bring me a 3-year-old heifer, a 3- year-old goat, a 3-year-old ram, a turtledove, and a young pigeon. Then he brought all these to him and cut them into two, down the middle, and placed each piece opposite the other.*

Not only did God cut covenant with Abraham by using animals; he also told Abraham to cut or circumcise himself which was the foreskin of his penis and the foreskin of the children. This cutting was the representation of blood shedding and now that Abraham was obedient, he was a marked man, and we see that Abraham did his part. But did God follow through with his part? Did God really give Abraham a son as he promised? Always remember, a covenant is a giving and receiving relationship. Have you ever been in a relationship where you always were the one giving? If so, that wasn't a healthy covenant relationship. You want to be on the receiving end as well. As you just read, we see Abraham giving to God through obedience. Let's continue to read and see if we can locate God giving Abraham what he promised him. Keep in mind what God has promised you. Have you received it yet? Have you been doing your part? Now look at Genesis 18:10-14,

*I'll certainly return to you according to the time of life, and behold, Sarah your wife shall have a son." Now Abraham and Sarah were old, Well advanced in age; and Sarah had passed the age of childbearing. Therefore Sarah laughed within herself, saying, "After I have grown old, Shall I have pleasure, my lord being old also?" And the Lord said to*

*Abraham, "Why did Sarah laugh, saying, 'Shall I surely bear a child, since I am old?' Is there anything too hard for the Lord? At the appointed time I'll return to you, according to the time of life, and Sarah shall have a son."*

Here is God showing up again to reconfirm the promise he made with Abraham by telling him, " I'm still going to do what I have promised you. It does not matter how old you and your wife are, although your wife is laughing at what I said that I'll do. There is absolutely nothing too hard for me to perform in your life."

Man of God, you may think it's too late for you to obtain what you have believed God for, but it's not! The world may be telling you that you cannot have this or do that, but God will intervene and do what man said that couldn't be done. Why? Because he said, "Is there anything too hard for the Lord"! You may be on a verge of a serious divorce and you're believing God for restoration! Is there anything too hard for the Lord? You or a loved one may have received some bad news from the doctor saying you are about or they are about to die soon. You just say, is there anything too hard for the Lord? You may think that you can't get your wife pregnant because of a birth defect or some other cause. How can that be true when God told you to be fruitful and multiply in his word? Is there anything too hard for the Lord? You may have an incurable disease! Is there anything too hard for the Lord? You may be in prison and the parole board has mentioned to you that there's no way out! Is there anything too hard for the Lord? You may be an ex-convict and no one wants anything to do with you. Family, friends and even the boss you had an interview with told you, "We cannot use you, because you have two felonies on your record."

Is there anything too hard for the Lord? You may be looking at foreclosure on your house or eviction from your apartment, and your business and dreams are about to fold. You just look deep down inside of yourself and realize that you are a child of the most High God! And when you really truly believe that, you'll stand on top of the highest skyscraper like King Kong and shout, "Is there anything too hard for the Lord?"

Every so often, after God has made you a promise, he'll do just about anything to keep your faith in him going. That's what covenant relationship is all about. When you get weak, God is there to strengthen you with his word. It is very vital that you, man of God, spend time with God by reading his word and praying. Although Abraham was old and appeared to have no more juice in him, he still believed God would do what he promised. Go to Romans 4:19-21,

*And not being weak in faith, he didn't consider his own body, already dead (since he was about a hundred years old). And the deadness of Sarah's womb. He didn't waiver at the promise of God through unbelief, but was strengthen in faith, giving glory to God. And being fully convinced that what he had promised he was also able to perform.*

In those three verses alone I can see four attributes that you, man of God, should have in order to see the manifestations of God's promise in your life:

1. Not weak in faith
2. Not wavering at the promises of God through unbelief
3. Strong in faith
4. Fully convinced

As you have already read, these are four attributes that Abraham operated under to see his dream come true. This even amazes me. I wonder how in the world Abraham, at the age of a hundred, got an erection when there was no Viagra in Abraham's days! What did he use to activate his physical body to obtain sexual performance? What was Abraham's power that he used to perform this miraculous act? It was faith! Faith in the covenant, the agreement, pledge, or vow that God made with him. Abraham obviously knew that faith without works is dead!

So every night or maybe three or four nights out the week Abraham would tell his wife, "Sweetheart, don't worry about washing the dishes tonight after dinner. I just want you to relax in the homemade pool I made just for you and take some fragrances and oils that I purchased for you on your 89th birthday and just rub it all over your beautiful wrinkled...I mean your beautiful smooth skin. When I get back from the river washing the dishes, I'd like to step back into the tent and see you lying there with your white lamb fur lingerie on and don't forget to wear those sexy goat skins that your handmaiden gave to you. After all, my beloved one, even though God promised me and you a son, 'Faith without works id dead!' and I don't mind doing the works!!!" (Ha, ha, ha)

You see, man of God, faith is simply acting on God's word. You have sixty-six books of God's covenant promises and when you do your part in order to obtain the promises you are operating by faith. Can you see another part of who you are! You have the power of faith inside you and when you live by those four attributes of a man of faith, you'll be like one of the heroes of faith in Hebrews chapter 11.

As you have already read, Abraham has been obedient to God, keeping his part of the covenant. Now let's read on and see if God did his part in what he promised Abraham and Sarah. Let's look at Genesis 21:1-7,

*And the Lord visited Sarah as he had said, and the Lord did for Sarah as he had spoken. For Sarah conceived and bore Abraham a son in his old age, at the set time of which God had spoken to him. And Abraham called the name of his son who was born to him–whom Sarah bore to him–Isaac. Then Abraham circumcised his son, Isaac, when he was eight days old, as God had commanded him. Now Abraham was one hundred years old when his son,*

*Isaac, was born to him. And Sarah said, "God has made me laugh, and all who hear will laugh with me." She also said, "Who would have said to Abraham that Sarah would nurse children? For I have borne him a son in his old age."*

Wow! God never ever fails! We see that he has kept his covenant with Abraham. Can you imagine how Abraham felt after he saw his very dream unfold in front of his eyes? He didn't care how old he was, he didn't focus on the doubts or the opinions of others. He stayed diligent in doing his part. He was tenaciously obedient towards God. Always keep this phrase in mind, "Your present obedience determines your future harvest." You are finding out  who you are by knowing God has made you to become a "covenant man." Before I wrap this chapter up, there's more that I want to share with you about becoming a mark-minded man. A man whose mind is marked by the covenant–agreement, pledge, or vow–created by God for your possession.

## Super Section Three: The attitude of a covenant man

Have you ever been in the middle of a lake, river, sea or ocean, in a boat, and you wanted to be still and keep the waves from rocking your boat? What did you or the captain of the boat do? I'd guess that you just let down the anchor of that boat. The purpose of the anchor was to keep you from wavering and losing your position in the area of the water that you'd like to maintain. This is a perfect example of how God wants your minds to be anchored in his covenant. He knows that once his covenant is anchored in your mind, you won't allow Satan to cause you to waver or lose your position as a strong Christian covenant man.

I know that you have heard such statements as, "Your attitude is everything!" and "Your attitude determines your altitude" a million times during your time on earth. Such statements are true! Your attitude *is* everything, and your attitude *does* determine how high in life you'll go.

We know that a covenant is a promise, pledge, agreement, or vow between two or more parties. We know that a covenant isn't a contract because a contract can be broken and a covenant cannot be broken when you make one with God. The moment you make a covenant with God, you are sealed or bound for life. We can break our part of the covenant when we don't do our part. It doesn't mean that the covenant as a whole is broken because of God's grace and mercy; he'll never violate his part. Therefore, when we don't do our part he is still there willing and waiting to do his part and is patiently waiting for us to do our part so that his covenant can be fulfilled on the earth. We also understand that a covenant can only be broken by death. We also learned that God does make a covenant with men and that Abraham was a man that God made covenant with. Abraham did his part and we see that God didn't lie. How do we know? Because he did his part and God cannot lie. Look at Psalm 89:34,

*My covenant I won't break, nor alter the word that has gone out of my lips.*

Now there's a scripture you can hold on to when you begin to doubt the promises of God's word in your life. I know that you are excited about learning another super power that you have inside you, but now I want to show you how to make the covenant of God work for you so that you can experience life-changing results. You may say, "That's simple! We just do our part of the covenant." And you're right! You may know you need to do your part, but *how* to do your part is totally different. I know in order to drive my car, I have to get in it and turn the ignition switch on, but do I know how exactly to do that? In certain cars, there's a peculiar way you turn on that particular car. This is why I have to look at the car's manual and learn how to do that. Doing your part is the correct way to turn your covenant on, but let's learn how and what supports the covenant that God made with you. The best way to show you is by looking into the word of God. I want to show you several men who possessed a covenant attitude, which is the key to how to get the covenant to work for you. Are you ready to discover some more about who you are in Christ? If so, let's go and get our power! Look with me at 2 Kings 20:1-6,

*In those days Hezekiah was sick and near death. And Isaiah the prophet, the son of Amos, went to him and said to him, "Thus says the Lord: set your house in order, for you shall die, and not live." Then he turned his face toward the wall. And prayed to the Lord saying, "Remember now, O Lord, I pray, how I have walked before you in truth and with a loyal heart, and have done what was good in your sight." And Hezekiah wept bitterly. And it happened, before Isaiah had gone out into the middle court, that the word of the Lord came to him saying, "Return and tell Hezekiah the Leader of my people, Thus says the Lord, the God of David your father, "I have heard your prayer, I have seen your tears; surely I'll heal you. On the third day you shall go up to the house of the Lord and I'll add to your days fifteen years. I'll deliver you and this city from the hand of the kind of Assyria; and I'll defend this city for my own sake, and for the sake of my servant David."*

Now, did you see that! How did this man, just like you and me, get God to move on his behalf? After God sent a prophet to basically tell him, "Hey, Mr. Hezekiah, God told me to come tell you that you need to call the whole family in so you can get your will together and to say your last good-byes because your end is near!" After hearing that bad news, can you imagine how Hezekiah felt? But let's look at how he responded to the bad news he received. In verse two, King Hezekiah, who was a godly king, turned his face to the wall and prayed. Prayed what? He prayed his covenant back to God. How? By opening up his mouth with a covenant-minded attitude by saying in verse three, "Wait a minute, God. Remember (which means covenant) how I have walked before you with a true and loyal heart and have done those things which are good and pleasing in your sight!"

You may say, "Why is this guy reminding God of his part and what he has done for God?" He has a right to remind God of the covenant he made with him. Just like when you hear bad news, you don't cave in and quit. That is the time you activate your super power, which is opening your mouth and declaring back to God what he has promised you! I can prove that this is your right. Look at Isaiah 43:26,

*Put me in remembrance; Let us contend together; state your case, that you may be acquitted.*

Put God in remembrance of what? His word! His word is his covenant and his covenant is his word. And we see King Hezekiah doing just that:

- Putting God in remembrance of his word
- Contending with God instead of giving upon God
- Stating his case

King Hezekiah did his part, and God did his part. How? By telling his prophet Isaiah, "Get off of interstate 3 going north and get on interstate 3 going south. Go back and tell my covenant partner I've heard his prayer. See, he has a covenant attitude instead of a fearful attitude. I won't allow him to die. In fact, I'll add to his days fifteen more years. I'll cause him to win the war and his enemies will become servants for my covenant partner, King Hezekiah."

Once again, how did Hezekiah get this to work? He possessed a covenant attitude and he knew who he was by speaking positive, faith-filled words, knowing that God had to do his part. Religious people may say, "Wait a minute; God does not have to do anything!!!" Oh yes, he does! Why? He made a covenant–promise, pledge, agreement, or vow–with you. And the Bible says there was no other he could swear by so he swore by himself, which means again that he cannot lie.

What would have happened if King Hezekiah hadn't been covenant-minded? Son of God, he'd have died! What have you allowed to die in your life? What dream or desire has died? Have you allowed your marriage to die? Have you allowed your fellowship with your child or children to die because of your selfishness? Have you allowed your fellowship time and relationship with God to die? If you have allowed anything to die that has godly benefits attached to it, here's some good news. God has a restoration covenant available for you. Look with me at Joel 2:21 and 25,

> Fear not, O land (you) be glad and rejoice, for the Lord has done marvelous things! So I'll restore to you the years that the swarming locust has eaten, the crawling locust, the consuming locust, and the chewing locust, my great army which I sent among you. You shall eat in plenty and be satisfied.

There's your covenant of restoration. If you have lost something, begin today by doing your part, which is found in verse 21:

- Fear not
- Be glad
- Rejoice

Do your part with a covenant-minded attitude, and you'll begin to see that God will really do his part and keep his word.

A superhero is known for facing challenges in all arenas of life. The true reason why King Hezekiah didn't die was because he knew exactly who he was. His heart was warmed by the fact he had a secure relationship with God. He understood that he and God were covenant partners. After King Hezekiah contended for his life and was graced to live another fifteen years, he then went into war with a covenant attitude knowing that God was going to cause him to win over the King of Assyria and his army. After it was all over, King Hezekiah was known to be a superhero in his kingdom. Are you known as a superhero? If not, begin to practice what you have learned about yourself. How? Speak out of your mouth that you are a covenant man and then, say and put it into action with an attitude that God, your covenant partner, is going to do his part as you continue to do your part.


# Super Section Four: Was it really a slingshot and a stone that killed him?


King David is one of my favorite Bible characters. King David was a superhero to the nation of Israel and even today he is still known as a man after God's own heart. When any man has a heart towards God, that man, too, will become a superhero because he knows the power that has been given to him.

After hearing the story of David and Goliath or watching a movie of it, have you ever wondered if it was really a stone launched by a slingshot that caused a giant to fall down and die? What really enabled this teenage boy to fearlessly run towards this giant and kill him? Well, I have discovered the key to David's victory. David experienced victory over a giant because he knew who he was! Who was David? Not only was he a man after God's own heart, he was a man who had a violent covenant attitude! He was a king and a warrior who almost never lost a war. Back in the day of Goliath's death, King Saul was king over Israel. After Goliath had made a bet with King Saul and all of Israel no one was up to meet the challenge. They were all terrified of the size of Goliath. Even the king was afraid. But David, a teenager at that time, came to King Saul and all those which were gathered around and made this statement. Look at 1 Samuel 17:26,

*Then David spoke to the men who stood by him, saying, "What shall be done for the man who kills this Philistine and takes away the reproach from Israel? For who is this uncircumcised Philistine, that he should defy the armies of the Living God?*

In other words, David came to them saying, If I kill this guy for you what's going to be my reward? David was no fool; he figured if he was going to put his life on the line for the king and the nation of Israel, he should get something for his heroic services. Verse twenty-six identifies the key to David's victory. He began looking at everyone, as they bowed their heads in defeat. David shouted a question to them, "Who is this uncircumcised Philistine?" In other words, who is this man who doesn't have a covenant with God, who's trying to kill the armies of the living God?

Do you remember when God told Abraham to circumcise every boy and by doing so they'd be in covenant with God? Well, Goliath was never in covenant with God, which means he was uncircumcised. David knew that he could take this guy out because he knew that Goliath wasn't in covenant with God and he knew that he, David, *was* in covenant with God. This gave him the confidence to defeat Goliath.

When a man has confidence, it can clearly be heard and seen. Just ask the guy who if even E.T. looked at him, would be terrified. Although this guy is ugly, he has one of the most beautiful women in the world. How? I used to ask the same question until I found the answer in the word of God in Hebrews 10:35,

*Therefore, don't cast away your confidence, which has great reward.*

As ugly as this guy was, he knew within himself that he could have anything he wanted! He was extremely confident in himself. When people told him that he was ugly, he just continued to look in the mirror every day and tell himself, "I look good today! I am a man on a mission. I am going somewhere in life. I am smart, bright and intelligent. I am also a man of responsibility. I have the ability to respond in every area of my life and the first beautiful woman that I'm attracted to I'll win her because I am somebody and I know that I got it going on!"

Can you hear the confidence in his words? Well, the Bible says, "You can have what you say." And this ugly fellow got what he said! The very next beautiful woman that he found attractive, he approached as smoothly as a smooth landing, and even though she saw a guy that looked like he was wearing a scary Halloween mask, she was somehow able to look past his ugliness. She saw and heard his confidence as he talked and walked with her through the city's finest mall. After a month or so, the ugliest guy in the city was walking with the prettiest girl in the city. She had her arm locked into his arm with balloons in the other hand; they were strolling down the long aisles of the finest mall in the city. This guy didn't throw away his confidence and for not doing so he received his reward, which was the prettiest woman in the city.

Man of God, you cannot ever lose in any arena of life when you operate in confidence. It will be sure to reward you. Keep in mind, men, confidence speaks and acts. It is the substance that will cause your covenant with God to manifest in your life. Look again with me in 1Samuel 17:45-46,

*Then David said to the Philistine, "You come to me with a sword, with a spear, and with a javelin, but I come to you in the name of the Lord of hosts, the God of the armies of Israel, whom you have defiled. This day the Lord will deliver you into my hand, and I'll strike you and take your head from you. And this day I'll give the carcasses of the camp of the Philistines to the birds of the air and the wild beasts of the earth, that all the earth may know that there is a God in Israel."*

Here's a short teenager, whose occupation was feeding and tending to sheep in the field, standing in front of a giant who happens to be the champion of the whole wide world. He opens his mouth and starts speaking to the giant by telling him what he is about to do to him, even before they threw the first punch! David said to him, "You come to me with a bunch of weapons, but I come to you with confidence in my covenant with God and this day the Lord will deliver you into my hands. And then I'll cut your head off when I knock you down and will show the whole earth how to get ahead in life by using the substance of confidence in the covenant that God has made with men." You see that confidence in your covenant will cause you to speak boldly! Look at 1 Samuel 17:48,

*Therefore, it was, when the Philistine arose and come and drew near to meet*

*David, that David hurried and ran toward the army to meet the Philistine. Then David put his hand in his bag and took out a stone; and he slung it and struck the Philistine in his forehead, so that the stone sank into his forehead, and he fell on his face to the earth.*

Did you notice that David hurried and ran to the giant! What actually motivated David to run towards the giant instead of David having second thoughts about his covenant right for victory and protection with God? It was his previous victories and protection. Look at 1Samuel 17:37,

*Moreover David said, "The Lord who delivered me from the paw of the lion and from the paw of the bear, he'll deliver me from the hand of the Philistine."*

You see, David had already had some victories stored up to remind him that God's covenant will always work for him as long as he had confidence, the force that will cause you to speak and act on what God has promised. Just to remind you, when David was born, he was circumcised. Just like you, he is the seed of Abraham. As far as David and Goliath, let's see if David received what he said. Look at 1 Samuel 17:51,

*Therefore David ran and stood over the Philistine, took his sword and drew it out of its sheath and killed him, and cut off his head with it. And when the Philistines saw that their champion was dead, they fled.*

Men that are covenant-minded always turn out to be champions in the battles of life. Just think how the children of Israel viewed the short teenager who fed the sheep in the field. After the defeat of the giant everyone was afraid of, they viewed David as a superhero, as he maintained his stance as a man in covenant with God. You, man of God, are a superhero, for he is inside of you. One of your purposes as a man of God is to maintain what your heavenly father has already obtained for you, and that is to have confidence in his covenant he has provided for you.

## Super Section Five: He Got in God's Face!

*You command me. (Isaiah 45:11)*

After reading the title of this section of the chapter, you may be wondering "Who is the person who got into God's face?" and "What gives him the right to get into the face of the Almighty God?" That statement does sound out of place. But what if I told you and showed you that you have every right to get into the face of God and command him to move and act out on what he has promised to you? When I first heard about this information existing in the Bible, it blew me away. I'll never forget when my spiritual father, Creflo Dollar, preached that message on a particular night during a Faith Convention that was held at World Changers Church International. He was teaching on the subject that you're reading about now, The Covenant–how to expand your capacity of faith. I just couldn't believe what he was saying although he was proving what he was teaching out the word of God. It was my religious upbringing that made the word of God of no effect. Sad to say, the religious demon is still hovering around in today's churches and in Christians. This could be one of the reasons why the body of Christ isn't experiencing the power that it should, because the word which power comes from isn't effective because of the deception of religious tradition.

It wasn't until I went home with my notes, the tape and my Bible, and dug deep into it to see if it was really real, that I saw it was as real as you are reading this book! I was a stranger to my covenant. No wonder I didn't see any victories like King Hezekiah and King David–I kept the superhero caged up inside me.

Superheroes are double darers. They are always up for the challenge. They seek justice when a situation is twisted and that's what this man did. He sought justice in a situation that sounded twisted. Who is this man, you may ask? I'll give you a hint. He is a leader that God raised up to lead his people out of bondage. You may say that's not much of a hint. After all, God has always used a man, a leader, to lead his people out of bondage. That's true, but this man saw God and got into his face. In order to do that, his relationship with God had to be tight! God longs to have the same experience with us. Who is this man? How did he get justice for his people that God had planned to kill?

Keep this fact in mind. In order for him to get into God's face, he had to know who he was. Read with me Exodus 32:7-14,

*And the Lord said to Moses, "Go get down! For your people whom you Brought out of the land of Egypt have corrupted themselves. They have turned aside quickly out of the way which I commanded them. They have made themselves a molded calf, and worshipped it and sacrificed to it, and said, 'This is your god, O Israel, that brought you out of the land of Egypt!'" And the Lord said to Moses, "I have seen this people, and indeed it is a stiff-necked people! Now therefore, let me alone, that my wrath may burn hot against them and I may consume them. And I'll make of you a great nation." Then Moses pleaded with the Lord his God, and said, "Lord, why does your wrath burn hot against your people whom you have brought out of the land of Egypt with great power and with a mighty hand? Why should the Egyptians speak, and say, he brought them out to harm them, to kill them in the mountains, and to consume them from the face of the earth? Turn from your fierce wrath, and relent from this harm to your people.*

*Remember Abraham, Isaac, and Israel, your descendant, and they shall inherit it forever." So the Lord repented from the harm which he said he'd do to his people.*

At this moment, you may find yourself scratching your head, wondering how in the world did one man that was created by the most high God, get God himself to repent or to change his mind! I mean, what gave Moses the right to question God and to even tell him what to do in verse 12 by telling God to stop being angry with the people, and by the way you need to repent, and God did it! Why? Look at verse 13–this is why. Moses stood before God Almighty and put him in remembrance of his word by reminding God of the covenant he made with Abraham, Isaac, and Jacob (who is also called Israel). And God remembered that he couldn't destroy the seeds of Abraham.

Why is it that we can see and hear Moses' confidence? Moses knew who he was, a covenant man with God! He had every right to go before God and ask him for anything and God had to respond to his covenant partner, Moses. But what if Moses had decided to walk out of the meeting he was having with God and go and join in with the rest of the children of Israel as they began to party, smoke a couple of joints, have unlimited sex, and worship other gods? Do you think God would have done his part by giving them a second chance? I personally don't think so. Why? If Moses would have had done so, he'd have violated his part of the covenant.

Do you think right now in your life you're where you are at because you have failed to do your part of the covenant? The most high God has promised you to be the head and not the tail, above and never beneath. You are supposed to be overcoming the world. You are supposed to have whatever you say. If you are married, your wife and children are supposed to be happy and glad to see you as an image of God. You are not supposed to be living from paycheck to paycheck. If you are in prison, you should not allow worry to torment you. It is only a negative form of meditation. Your trust should be in God, not in the parole board, for *The king's heart is in his hands (Proverbs 21:1).*

There are so many covenant promises that you have not experienced. Why? What's holding you back? Is it the pride of life, the lust of the flesh, or the lust of the eyes? If so, rededicate your life to God and if you're not a Christian yet, what a great place to start while you are discovering yourself as a covenant man. What a great privilege to have God as a covenant partner. A God that will be more than delighted for you to get in his face and command him for whatever the need may be. Covenant attitude develops when you're confident that God will do his part as long as you are doing your part. There are people waiting that only you can touch and reach out to. Success will come your way as a result of sowing your time and energy displaying your covenant attitude. One day, people will walk up to you and ask how you do what you do.

You'll say with confidence, "I found out who I am. I am a covenant man and I got in God's face."

## Super Section Six: Now I know

Those were a few superheroes in the Bible who had the covenant of God tattooed on their minds and hearts. These were men of God just like you and me. We have the same opportunities they had to operate in the covenant. God isn't a respecter of persons, but he is a respecter of faith! What he did for one man, God can do for another man, only if that man (which is you) will begin to find out what the other man did to get what he got! Abraham, King Hezekiah, King David, and Moses were men who experienced great victories throughout their lives. They were all superheroes. The man that was within, which was their spirit, wasn't asleep. They knew who they were, when they discovered that God offered to make a covenant with them. Take advantage of those examples–it will give great recompense (payback) if you'll practice what you find out.

I started this chapter with Abraham, and I'd like to close it with Abraham, the father of faith. It was his faith in the covenant promises God made with him. Although Abraham knew who he was and received his promises from God through faith, God wanted to prove to Abraham exactly where his heart was, and God wanted to know as well. Could it be, man of God, that the blessing of God has been paralyzed in your life because your heart is somewhere other than in the hands of God?

God wants to be number one in your life, not number two or three. He is a jealous God! Have you ever wondered why God is jealous and yet an unconditional loving father towards us? His jealousy isn't based on fear. It comes from love. The reason why God desires to be number one in your life is because he knows what's best for you. He knows the results of sin in your life and he knows the results of obedience in your life. He knows you better than you know yourself. That's why he put the desire in my heart to write this book so that you and every other man that reads this book can discover yourselves.

Just think about this for a moment, those of you that have children. You love your child or children, and you know that there is no hate or fear in your heart towards them. You know you want to give them the best. You also know that you'd like to be first in their lives. How would it make you feel if your son or daughter or kids went to their uncle first for help instead of coming to you? That, my friend, would make you jealous! I guarantee it. It's a jealousy motivated by love, knowing that you want your child or children to come to daddy first! Not second or third, but first!!! Well, son of God, that's how God feels about you. So if you haven't realized it yet, God is testing you. Not until a man's heart, which is his spirit man, is pumping in the hand of God will that man begin to find himself. This will qualify him to go to the next level of blessings God has stored up in a huge barn labeled "your possessions in your destiny." He did it for Abraham and he can do it for you. Look with me at Genesis 22:1-3,

*Now it came to pass after these things that God tested Abraham, and said to him, "Abraham!" and he said, "Here I am." Then he said, take now your son, your only son Isaac, whom you love, and go to the land of Moriah, and offer him there as a burnt offering on one of the mountains of which I shall tell you." So Abraham rose early in the morning and saddled his donkey, and took two of his young men with him, and Isaac his son; and he split the wood for the burnt offering, and arose and went to the place of which God had told him.*

God is telling Abraham to go to a mountain and kill the son that he promised him. In verse three, Abraham promises God that he'll obey Him. "I'll be on my way, my son and I will go to the mountain. I'll do as you ask, Lord. I'll take my son's life, just as you asked." Not one time did you hear Abraham questioning God's instructions. I don't know about you, but if God had asked me to do that to my child, I'd have at least asked him what's going on before I followed through. Remember, it's a test. God could very well be asking for a habit instead of a child, or a career opportunity, a mate, or whatever it may be that has your heart. This didn't matter to Abraham because he gave God plain old simple obedience. Why did he obey God's instructions without second-guessing? Look at Genesis 22:5,

*And Abraham said to his young men, "Stay here with the donkey; the lad (son) and I'll go yonder and worship, and we'll come back to you."*

Here's Abraham telling the young men he brought with him as they approached the mountain, stay here while my son and I go on top of this mountain and obey God (which means worship), and my son and I will return to you again. If I was there, I'd have told Abraham, "What do you mean, you and your son will be coming back? God told you to go on top of the mountain and kill your son! So the only one that will be coming down from the mountain will be you!"

Abraham didn't care what it looked like or sounded like. He knew who he was by being in covenant with God. His confidence that supported his covenant produced a covenant attitude, which said, "I don't care if God kills him or not–he promised me this son of mine and if he decides to kill him, God will have to raise him back up!" Therefore, he was confident that he was going to meet the boys with his son right there by his side.

Now as Abraham and his son Isaac were on their way to the top of the mountain where burnt offerings were sacrificed, Isaac asked his father a question in verse seven. He basically said, "My father, I know that you told me to come with you to this burnt offering ceremony and I see the fire and the wood, but where is the lamb?" and Abraham said, "You're the one I'll be offering a burnt sacrifice today!" Just kidding ha, ha, he really didn't say that. This is what he really did say in verse eight, "My son, God will provide himself a lamb for the burnt offering." Now I know that you had to pick upon that statement. Once again, here is Abraham speaking with such confidence that God will present his own burnt offering instead of his son, knowing that God told him to kill his son for a burnt offering. Man of God, please pay attention to the words that came out of Abraham's mouth. You see them forming from his imagination. Abraham imagined first that God was going to provide something else instead of his son. He perhaps imagined a lamb and his words caught up with the image that he had and then, he spoke those words with confidence! The Bible does say in Proverbs 12:14,

*A man will be satisfied with good by the fruit of his mouth.*

However, let's see if Abraham was satisfied with the image that he had of his son being kept back from death. In verse nine, Abraham still followed through on the instructions that were given to him. Abraham was extremely obedient to God. That was his part of the covenant. If you'll become extremely obedient towards God, he'll be extremely obedient to your command, which is his part of the covenant with you. So in verse ten, Abraham picked up his knife, stretched forth his hands with tears in his eyes, but still confident. As he started to thrust the knife into his son, an Angel of the Lord in verse eleven showed up and said, "Abraham! Abraham! Don't kill your son for the Lord. The Lord says you don't have to do any harm to the son I promised you. For now I know that I am first place instead of your son." And when he heard those words from God, he first gave glory to God and grabbed his son, and he was greatly satisfied because of the good that came out of his mouth. Words of faith instead of words of fear, doubt, and unbelief! Did that image Abraham had line up with what he imagined in verse thirteen? Abraham lifted up his eyes and saw a ram–not a lamb, but a ram–something bigger and better than a lamb. Abraham offered up the ram for a burnt offering instead of his promised son. Now what about the two young men waiting on Abraham and his son? Look at Genesis 22:19,

*So Abraham returned to his young men, and they arose and went together to*

I can say that those young men were standing in awe as they saw with their own eyes that what Abraham said out of his mouth came to pass. Because of that, they knew Abraham wasn't the average man. They saw him display his power! What power? The power to call those things that are not as though they were, to be able to see what he called that wasn't yet in reality, the power of seeing the reality of his image that he had manifested. Now that's power! Abraham was a superhero in the eyes of those young men and his son Isaac by having confidence in his covenant, which saved Isaac's life. He is a superhero to us because his example gives us hope to do what he did in the times of testing and trials. So God can say to you, "Now I know."

Not only was it Abraham who had an image of his son being raised from the dead or a lamb being offered instead. God saw his image and got an image for himself. God knew after the first Adam had failed that he had to find another Adam to accomplish what the first Adam couldn't accomplish because of sin. After the fall of man, Satan had stolen the keys from the first Adam. The keys of the first Adam were designed for you and me. Those keys consist of your authority and dominion that God gave to us through the first Adam.

As God began to meditate on the image that Abraham had, God begin to get a blueprint on how to snatch the keys that Satan had stolen. He was eager and willing to do anything to get back what rightfully belonged to us as his sons and with that willing attitude he decided to sacrifice his only son for us all. How? By nailing him to the cross, whipping him with the cat of nine tails—which snatched the skin off his very back, driving huge stake nails into his hands and placing not the average Nike headband on his head but a crown of thorns. Blood was everywhere; Jesus looked like sin, ugly! He had to look like sin in order to get through the gates of hell! I mean just think about it. Do you think God's security forces—strong, big, powerful angels—are going to let you go through the pearly gates to enter the presence of God looking like sin? Just as Satan disguised himself as a snake to get into the Garden of Eden, Jesus was disguised as sin to get beyond the gates of Hell. After he did so, he finally found Satan, crushed his head, and took back the keys. After three days and three nights, God raised him back up again from the dead. Jesus came back to the earth, shocking all that knew Him. He told them to get rid of their sinful nature, He said he'd paid the price to wash away their sins with His blood. He also promised to give them the key to all power on this earth. Jesus Christ our Lord and Savior was called the Lamb of God.

Everything worked out as God planned. Jesus was the second and last Adam. He was the very blueprint that God imagined from the image of Abraham. By the resurrection of Jesus, he has created a new covenant for us, a better covenant that has better benefits! We no longer have to kill animals to make a covenant with God. You may be asking, how *do* you make a covenant with God? If you have already made Jesus Christ your Lord and Savior over your life, you have just made a covenant–a promise, pledge, or agreement–with God Almighty. Now that you are in covenant with God, you have a right to partake in all Jesus had: his authority, his character and his inheritance. Abraham inherited much, which qualifies you to his inheritance. Abraham received all the promises of God through faith. Every promise of God has been made available for you. Why? In Galatians 3:29 it states,

*And if you are Christ's then you are Abraham's seed, and heirs according to the promise.*

You have made the Lord Jesus Christ your savior, right? So you are part of the stars that Abraham couldn't number in Genesis 15 when God said he'd give Abraham a seed (Isaac) that would outnumber the stars in the sky. In addition, it is true today that any man who accepts Jesus is another seed of Abraham–and that, my friend, could very well outnumber the stars. Now that you know that you are a seed of Abraham, you have a covenant right to possess all of the promises of God that lie waiting in your Bible. Remember as you look into the promises of God in your Bible, it will always show God's part–what he'll do for you, and your part–what you'll have to do in order to obtain God's marvelous promises.

You have just discovered another attribute of who you really are, another power that is inside of you once you come into the kingdom of God. You are a covenant man. Do your part, men! Believe it or not, the kingdom of darkness is waiting for some superheroes that are produced by God–and that is what you are. There are no more excuses! Men, when you know you have a covenant with God, there is absolutely nothing on the face of this planet that can stop you! Go! I repeat, go! Begin doing your part, so God can do his part. You'll both become one as He displays his superpower. You'll become the superhero God chose you to be a covenant marked, covenant-minded man.

GO WIN!

Dear Hero,

Man its hot in here! It's now the month of July and there are no air conditions here at Rivers State Prison. This prison is an old morgue! Everything on the inside of it is concrete; when you walk on the floor it's hot! When you stand up against the wall it's hot! 8 people alone have been rushed to the hospital because of dehydration and asthma attacks! It's extremely so hot and humid in this cage that I feel like I'm going to die. Not only am I hot physically I'm hot emotionally! Why? Because my counselor just called me into her office and gave me some bad news. She said that the parole board has moved my release date from Sept 8, 2005. I asked why? She said she did not know. I then got so upset!!! Who wouldn't! I can't sleep at night from smoke from other men smoking there cigarettes. I'm coughing 24/7 while I'm trying to maintain my concentration as I write this book to you. Before I received my bad news I almost got into a fight! But I didn't loose my cool I just simply walked in love. Guys have discovered I can write so now I have to take time out to write letters for judges, home goings and cards. I work 8 hours Monday thru Fridays shaking doo-doo off nasty towels and sheets from old folk's nursing home. I work out a lot to keep myself in shape. Man I'm hurt and mad. I just came in from running on the yard just to hear that the showers are not working. All kinds of thoughts are circling around my head. One main thought is I want to give up writing this book! It's a waste of time, who is going to read a book written in prison. Yea I know people in the bible did, but so what I'm not them. I'm still mad right now! I've got to spend an extra five months in this hot gutter! But you know what man I'm not going to quit, I refuse to be selfish. I will get my mind off me and get it back on you. I can't let you down! No matter what the conditions are. Ouch! It's so painful; oh I forgot to mention I have an upset tooth that the Dentist won't be able to pull it out until next Thursday! Until then I got to walk around with a painful mouth plus it's hot. I just finished chapter 5 and have five more chapters to go. Thank god for mama she just sent me 50 dollars on my books. I have a new pen to write with and 3 tablets of paper to write on. I'm going to suck it up! This is painful! But I can make it! Although I feel like throwing in the white towel I won't. Why! Because I can't give up on you. OK Chapter 6 lets begin.

BROOKS

# Chapter Six

## Super Section One: You are authorized to dominate!

*You have made him to have dominion over the works of your hands;*
*you have put all things under his feet.(Psalm 8:6)*

The word "dominate" is a very strong, powerful word. According to Webster's New World Dictionary, the word "dominate" means donimus, a master, to rule or control by superior power, to rise above the surrounding. It is a demanding word, which seems to fit into every category that life brings. In the sports category, you have Michael Jordan, who dominated the game of basketball. He is known to be the best player that has ever played in the history of the NBA! What actually made Michael Jordan the best ever? Simple–he dominated the court. He was and still is basketball superhero. Football is my favorite sport. Deion Sanders dominated the whole football field as a cornerback. Sunday after Sunday, year after year, he just did his job, covering his opponent like chocolate frosting covers a cake. His God-given ability helped make him the NFL's best cornerback. In the sport of boxing, Muhammad Ali, Evander Holyfield and Mike Tyson also dominated in the ring. Babe Ruth, Hank Aaron and Sammy Sosa dominated the baseball diamond, while Wayne Gretzky dominated the ice. All of them have dominated their respective sports, because they were sure of their skills.

How about the animal kingdom? A dog can dominate a cat. A shark can dominate a jellyfish. A lion is the boldest and ferocious creature in the jungle. It is known as the king of all and can dominate all the kingdom of wildlife. Light dominates over darkness. A jet airplane dominates over a little sailboat. The father's blood dominates the mother's blood, when a newborn child enters into this world. In the category of music, hardcore rock, gangsta rap, and R & B that dishes out lyrics of drugs, violence, the degrading of women, and sexual motivation seems to be the golden key that Satan is using to dominate today's kids, teenagers, and young adults throughout the land. What's sad about this is that the world is dominating the Christians!

Look at the dope dealers who pull up next to a Christian at the red light in their big Mercedes with shining, expensive rims, while you're sitting in your little Volkswagen with a "Jesus wants to bless your life" bumper sticker. You only have one hubcap on one tire of your car. Their music sounds better than yours. They dress better than you do. They seem to have more fun than you do. To sum it all up the sinners are dominating the Christians in every area of life. I know that may be hard to swallow, but it's the honest to God truth. It's even hard for me to swallow!

Let me ask you this question, "Have you ever honestly asked yourself, 'Why am I a man of God and a man of the world seems to be successful in all that he does? Here I am praying, fasting and confessing God's word, staying away from all of those beautiful women to have sex with, going to church and so on; and still they appear to be the blessed instead of me!'" If so, you're not alone, because I used to ask the same question until I received revelation from God while in prison. On that day, I believed God was allowing me to see things in a different perspective which was, in the case of sinners, they dominate in everything that they do whether it's music, entertainment such as comedy, acting, sports, or even in the field of entrepreneurship. In other words, they have found out a part of who they are, or I should say a fruit that came from the root.

You see, man of God, God has given every man talents and gift. Once you locate them it's just like locating another part of who you are. One problem that has occurred in the life of a man is after finding that talent or gift you define your whole identity in that instead of understanding that this is my gift, but not who I am. Remember, the foundation of a man's life knows who he really is in Christ. That is the objective of the Christian.

On the other hand, the sinner finds his gifts and talents that God has given him, but then Satan comes along and twists them, and causes that man to work for him as he dominates in the world with the gift that God has given him. But in actuality, Satan's major plan is to dominate *them* in the long run. Remember, he comes to kill, steal, and destroy.

For example, the guy you knew in the church choir or have heard about, that he was gifted to sing but when he got old enough he was all of a sudden singing R&B throughout the world like, "Baby this, baby that. Let me freak you, etc." While he was at church before then, singing words of encouragement, lifting someone up when they came through the door burdened down. While they're dominating in their gift, you eventually hear how strung out they are on drugs or how big of a financial bind they're in, and how they're about to lose everything. When I first began to see this, that's when God dropped it on me. He said, "Son, people who are sinners are dominating with a twisted gift. They are empowered by the suggestions of the enemy, they know who they are and they work hard with the principles that I have established in my word such as diligence, faithfulness, and commitment. They are faithful in whatever they do. They are diligent in whatever they do. They are committed to making that enticing music, telling those nasty jokes, and faithful in making those drug sales or whatever. They're winning! They're dominating! They're in first place! They are successful for a season. Why? Because they know who they are, and this causes them to dominate!

Now here's another big question for you. Why are you not dominating on this planet? Better yet, ask yourself, "Am I dominating or am I losing in life?" You may not have known it, but God put you here on the earth to dominate. You, Man, are a fascinating creature. You're a very unique creature. In fact, the angels in heaven questioned God himself about you. They asked (look with me in Psalm 8:4),

*What is man that you are mindful of him?*

Wow! Did you see that? In other words, here are the angels standing before God Almighty asking him a question about you! Not only that; according to the main scripture heading underneath the title of this chapter, the angels also refer back to God by speaking Psalm 8:6, which again says,

*You have made him (you) to have dominion over the works of your hands; you have put all things under his feet.*

Isn't that something? Men walk around not knowing who they are, while the angels know exactly who we are. I never personally have seen an angel, but if I ever do I know that I'd be in awe! It probably would be a breathtaking moment. But, according to those two scriptures we've read, when the angels look at you, they feel the same way.

You are a man God created and placed on this earth to dominate in every area of your life. God has given you dominion over everything that he has created and has put everything under your feet. When God said in Genesis 1:26 and 28, "Let us make man in our image and our likeness", he was talking about you and me. You may say, of course he said that, everybody knows that! Well, if so, why are men still failing in life instead of being like God, a winner? God even mentions twice in Genesis 1:26 and 28, "let them have dominion" on this earth. Adam was the first man given this privilege to dominate with God's power here on the earth, but he failed at do so! Why? Because of disobedience, which is caused by sin.  And sin, after it has run its course, will soon bring forth a curse. But here's good news: when you don't live a disobedient lifestyle and don't practice sin, you'll never have to worry about having a curse because in Galatians 3:13 it reads,

*Christ has redeemed us (you and me) from the curse of the law, having become a curse for us (for it is written, "curse is everyone who hangs on a tree"), that the blessing of Abraham might come upon the Gentiles in Christ Jesus, that we*

*might receive the promise of the spirit through faith.*

Just like Adam failed, there are many men right now in society failing. Notice I said failing, a continuous effort and not the word failure. Because you are prone to fail and miss the mark, and sometimes not all failure is bad. Because at times you have to fail before you can prevail and excel. Be extra careful what you call failure; it could be the very cable to jump-start you to success.

Although Adam failed in the garden, and his authority to dominate was stripped from him, it wasn't over in God's eyes. You see, Son of God, He's always looking for a man that he can use, someone with a sincere heart. You, reading this book, I want you to read this scripture. It's just for you. Look with me at 2 Chronicles 16:4 ,

*For the eyes of the Lord run to and from throughout the whole earth, to show himself strong on behalf of those whose heart is loyal to him.*

Adam wasn't the only man that God used in a mighty way. God found Noah, Abraham, Joseph, Moses, Joshua, King David, Solomon and the prophet Elisha, all the way up to Jesus Christ, his only begotten son. And it didn't even stop with Jesus. God found Peter, Paul, Smith Wigglesworth, Kathryn Kuhlman, Oral Roberts, the late Kenneth Hagin, Kenneth Copeland, Jerry Seville, Jesse Duplantis, T. D. Jakes, Leroy Thompson, Reinhart Bunke, R. W. Schambach, my spiritual father and hero, Creflo A. Dollar, of course me–Keith Lyvell Brooks—and, last but definitely not least, you! Yes, that's right, I said you! All of those men who were just mentioned were loyal to God and why He has shown himself strong in their lives and ministries. They all have been or still are dominating throughout the whole earth. So, as you can see, it just didn't stop at Adam.

Yes, we know and have just read that God created us to dominate, and it is a proven fact that there are still examples of men of God dominating throughout the land today. It is also good to know, based on the word of God, that you are discovering who you are by finding out in this chapter and this particular book that you are a man that's been placed on this earth to dominate, sealed and authorized to do so by God Almighty.

These men that God has used in a mighty way all have one thing in common. It is the stuff where their force of domination comes from, and without this stuff, there is no domination. Without this stuff, there is no authority. Without this stuff, there is absolutely no victory.

Some transportation requires an engine. For example, what good is a car without an engine, or perhaps an airplane–how can it be effective without an engine? Look at the space shuttle. If those two rockets are not attached to the shuttle, how could it launch off the launching pad and dash into space?

Everything in life has a support system. Without support, nothing works! Man of God, if you have children in a marriage or out of wedlock, those children need your support! Support your children; be a father just like God is towards you, even as he is supporting you! How? You are breathing, right? Without the support of people going into shopping centers and purchasing items, how could that shopping center last? What good is a school or a university without the support of books? What good is the Christian lifestyle without the force of love? You'll never be effective without the love of God in your life. God, who is love, is the root to your authority to dominate.

The stuff that I'm talking about, that support gives strength to your authority to dominate that all those great men of God used, is the anointing.

## Super Section Two: So you want the signature that will authorize you to dominate!

*It shall come to pass in that day that his burden will be taken away from your shoulder, and his yoke from his neck, and the yoke will be destroyed because of the anointing oil.*

When you sign your name on a document, across that is a sign of finalization whether it be a contract or some other legal form. Whenever you write your signature on something, you are saying, I agree; it's a done deal. Those great men and women of God were all filled with the Holy Spirit and were vessels that carried a very high dosage of God's anointing and supporting power. You may say, well, I'm no preacher, teacher or world-renowned evangelist. That power only belongs to them. In a sense, you are right! They are out there doing something, impacting the world in whatever area God called them to be in, so God had to display that power to them. For if they were not doing anything for God, what good would the power to dominate be. It would be useless!

So ask yourself this question, "Am I doing what God called me to do so that I can have his power to dominate?" God has a plan just for you. Those men and women of God are not the only ones he wants to use mightily on this earth. You have the same power in you, which is the anointing to dominate. You may say to yourself, "But how do I know that I have this power inside me to dominate?" The answer is simple. The day you received Jesus Christ into your life was the day that the anointing to dominate moved inside of you. You see, the word Christ in the Hebrew language means Messiah, which means the "anointed" or "the anointed one." The word "anoint" actually means to pour on, smear all over, or to rub into, like you rub lotion into a dry area of your body.

The anointing is the burden-removing, yoke-destroying power of God that is inside of you right now. Allow me to prove this to you. Oh, by the way, remember you are finding out who you are and learning that you have another form of power to operate under as a superhero! Look with me at Colossians 1:27,

*Christ in you, the hope of glory.*

Do you remember what Christ means? That's right, the anointed one. The burden-removing, yoke-destroying power of God! So, if the scripture just said, "Christ in you is the hope of glory," that means promising your heart to Christ gives you the burden-removing, yoke-destroying power of God, which would be your hope and glory to dominate here on this earth. Are you starting to realize who you are? Jesus Christ, the anointed one, the one with the burden-removing, yoke-destroying power of God, is living inside of you! You are a child of God, which makes God your father and Jesus Christ, the anointed one, your big brother.

Whenever you are birthed into a family, you automatically become an heir of that family. Since Jesus is now your Lord and Savior over your life, that gives you a right to operate under his power. Look at Romans 8:17,

*And if children, then heirs–heirs of God and joint heirs with Christ (the anointed one and his burden-removing, yoke-destroying power of God.).*

You are a joint heir with Christ, and since you are a joint heir with Christ, you can do what he did on this planet. He told you that you could do even greater works than he did! Now that's powerful!!! Please understand that Jesus wasn't talking about you coming up with something new. Just think with me, what else could you come up that's better than raising the dead? What Jesus was saying is, "I only had three years to dominate over sickness, disease, blindness, and poverty. So what I'm going to do is leave my power with you as I abide in you and you go out for the next thirty years and dominate just like I did. And as you lay hands on the sick and even raise the dead and dominate over the darkness in the world today, you'll find yourself doing greater works than your big brother, Jesus.

You are a very powerful man! Jesus wasn't a failure, and since you now know that you are anointed, why continue to fail in life? What are the circles that you are standing in right now? What are the bondages that seem to be holding you back? What are the addictive behaviors that you just can't seem to let go of? Let them go! You can break free from that mess, save yourself by tapping into that power that is inside of you.

How do you tap into the power? By opening your mouth and speaking over your life. Say over and over again, "I am anointed! I am anointed! I have the power! I have the power! I am delivered! I am delivered! I cannot be stopped!" The more you speak positive words over your life, the more those words will get into your heart and you'll begin to believe them. When you believe in something, you know exactly what's next! You act on what you believe, and the next thing that you know, you'll be delivered and be a new, free, powerful and strong man of God, who is now qualified to go out and save others. This makes you a superhero. All because you found out who you are, a man who is anointed to be authorized to dominate on this planet.

# Super Section Three: The six traits that you have in him

*I am the vine, you are the branches. He who abides in me, and I in him, bears much fruit; for without me you can do nothing. (John 15:4)*

Earlier, in Chapter Two, you read how mothers, aunts, uncles, brothers, sisters or close friends continually preach to you that you are just like your daddy! You walk like him. You talk like him. You look just like him. Most of those statements are extremely negative in most men's lives, such as, "Your daddy was a cheater and so will you be. Your daddy was abusive and you are too! Your daddy never had anything in life and his destiny was a non-productive lifestyle! Your daddy was stupid, slow, full of anger and ungrateful. It's no surprise that you are just like him."

All statements, whether they are positive or negative, if true, are nothing but traits that you picked up from the bloodline of your father. You may be saying, "Yes! I am doing exactly what my father was doing when he was my age. Yes! Whenever I look into the mirror I see the "look a like" traits that my father has given to me." You may be even aware that you don't want to be like your father. You want to kill this cycle of the curse that seems to be stamped on every generation of your father's bloodline. You want to destroy this curse once and for all so that it won't affect the next generation that has already been born through you or the seeds that are inside of you. Thank God that you are reading a book that was written in him. You have learned or been reminded that you are highly anointed by God. You know that you have the burden-removing, yoke-destroying power of God inside you to change and rearrange things in your everyday life. You now know that you have the ability to take authority of your dominating force that God has given you, supported by the anointing inside you.

You are in Christ, the anointed one, and he abides inside of you. He's in you! When you truly believe that, nothing and no one will be able to stop you! Why? Because God is in you, therefore, since Jesus who is the "anointed one" lives in you, you no longer have to walk around with your earthly father's traits. I'm not talking about your father's physical traits that will never change. If you look like him, there's nothing that you can do about that. I'm talking about his spiritual traits, the traits that you *can* do something about. If they are negative, here's more good news. When you abide in Christ (the anointed one) and he abides in you, you both become united as one.  1 Corinthians 6:17 says,

*But he who is joined to the Lord is one spirit with him.*

You can compare your relationship with the anointed one to Cookies-n-Cream ice cream. The cookies are in the ice cream and the ice cream in the cookies.  They are mixed together to produce Cookies-n-Cream ice cream, and the power of that ice cream is its cool refreshing taste. But there are traits that cause the ice cream to have flavor, and for it to be effective in the lives of people, traits such as sugar, milk, cookies, a mixing bowl, a freezer, spoons, bowls and cones are added. When all of these traits are joined together, you have the ice cream and the proper utensils that go with the ice cream. When you are joined together as one with Christ, you'll soon begin to get rid of the bad traits of your earthly father and begin to pick up the traits of your heavenly father. That's what I'm about to tell you about, the traits that you have when you're in him.

Who is in him? Jesus Christ, the anointed one and his anointing. You are about to discover seven more anointed traits that are inside you right now if you are a born-again believer. And if you are not born again, I want to inspire you to be born again as soon as possible. Superheroes have super traits; Jesus was and still is super, so when you are united with him, his super hops on your natural ability, which produces supernatural ability. It is another name for the anointing, the burden-removing, yoke-destroying power of God. Now let's begin to look at some traits of the anointing of Jesus which reside in you. There are seven facets of the anointing, or in other words, there are seven abilities that are birthed out of the anointing. They can be found in Isaiah 11:2,

*The spirit of the Lord shall rest upon him. The spirit of wisdom and understanding, the spirit of counsel and might, the spirit of knowledge and of the fear of the Lord.*

Notice how it reads that the spirit of the Lord shall rest upon him. Another name for spirit is the anointing, especially when it can get upon someone. Remember, the word anoint means to rub on, smear all over or to pour on. Now let's take all seven abilities and break them down so that your understanding can be enhanced.

- The anointing of wisdom is the ability to know what to do when you don't know what to do.
- The anointing of understanding is the ability to know and understand how to see things in a clearer view, what others cannot understand. While others try to figure out what's going on, you'll simply just understand.
- The anointing of counsel is the ability to give sound advice from the wisdom of God. When others don't know what to do or how to handle a situation. You'll be able to give wise information that will help and support others.
- The anointing of might is the ability to do what you couldn't do in the natural. A supernatural substance that will get all over you will cause the impossible to be possible in every area of life.
- The anointing of knowledge is the ability to have valid information from God, stored up in the inside of you. Ready to fire away when you need or others need to know a thing.
- The anointing of the fear of the Lord is the ability to reverence and respect God in difficult situations.
- The spirit of the Lord will empower you to get results.

You have just read that you have seven different types of anointing living inside you as a born again believer. There is once again another way of God showing you who you really are in Christ! Just think about that and begin to meditate (to roll over in your mind) on the fact that you have the ability to counsel, you have knowledge, and you can understand all things. You have the wisdom of God when you don't know what to do. You have the ability of might, strength that comes from God to do any and everything, and last but not least, you have the fear of the Lord.

Now I'm not talking about a worldly type of fear, because that fear leads to death! Most Christians believe that the fear of the Lord means that you have to walk around and be scared or terrified by God. Listen, men of God, God loves you and he is 100% in love with you. So, why would you walk around afraid that God is going to hurt you or bring some type of pain to you, when he promised you that no weapon formed against you shall prosper (Isaiah 54:11)? This tells me, and should tell you, that he is always protecting us.

For those who are or desire to be parents, how would it make you feel if your kids or child felt terrified and scared to ask you for anything, and every time they saw you they would run hide somewhere as you try to give them hugs and gifts to show how much you love them? For most men, that's how they treat God. Why? Because of old traditional thinking! You probably were brought up in a church where the preacher preached to you that God was going to get you if you did something wrong, or your mama or uncle said to you, "You didn't go to church. God isn't going to bless you!" This type of thinking will always tie the hands of God from blessing you as he desires. Why? You are motivated by fear instead of faith. Fearing the Lord means having **respect** for God. You'd want your child or children to respect you, right? That's what God wants from you. Not only that, but you have an anointing to respect the Lord. And when you find yourself about to do something that you shouldn't do and don't want to do, the anointing of the fear of the Lord will kick in to pull you out of that situation. In other words, you won't do this or that because you'll respect the Lord. Meditate on that! That should take care of the false religious and traditional thinking.

Let's begin to look at a couple of men of God who operated under the seven anointings that were made available for them in their time of need. Remember, the men in the Bible and their heroic experiences are vital examples for us to follow. God isn't a respecter of persons, but he is a respecter of faith. What he did for one man, he definitely can do for another who does the same thing that the first man did. I'm about to show you a man named Solomon, who had a great supply of the wisdom of God. He simply asked God for wisdom, and God gave it to him. You and I can do the same. God will give you wisdom, but you'll have to make a demand for it to come forth. And what is that demand? Faith! Look at James 1:5-6,

*If any of you lacks wisdom, let him ask of God, who gives to all liberally and without reproach, and it will be given to him. But let him ask in faith, with no doubting.*

How can you get the anointing of wisdom that's inside you to come forth? Simple–speak faith. Are you currently in a tight situation? Perhaps you have gotten yourself in some deep trouble and you don't see any way out. If this is you, go ahead and ask God with faith-filled words so that the wisdom inside you can be drawn out to handle whatever that task may be. In order to get water out of a well, you are going to have to pump and pump until the water comes exploding out to meet that need. Remember, pump faith-filled words out of the well of your heart and the anointing of wisdom will come upon you like it did for

Solomon in times when he didn't know what to do. His faith enabled him to depend on the wisdom of God, which always gave him victory. Now go to 1 Kings 3:16-28. Let's look at an example of the anointing of wisdom working through Solomon.

*Now two women who were harlots came to the king, and stood before him. And one woman said, "O my Lord, this woman and I dwell in the same house; and I gave birth while she was in the house. Then it happened, the third day after I gave birth, that this woman also gave birth. And we were together; no one was with us in the house, except the two of us in the house. And this woman's son died in the night, because she lay on him. So she arose in the middle of the night and took my son from my side, while your maidservant slept, and laid him in her bosom. And when I arose in the morning to nurse my son, there he was, dead. But when I examined him in the morning, indeed, he wasn't my son whom I had borne." Then the other woman said, "No! But the living one is my son," and the first woman said, "No! But the dead one is your son, and the living one is my son." Thus, they spoke before the king. And the king said, "The one says, this is my son and the other says, 'No! But your son is the dead one, and my son is the living one.'" Then the king said, "Bring me a sword." So they brought a sword before the king. And the king said, "Divide the living child in two, and give half to one, and half to the other." Then the woman whose son was living spoke to the king, for she yearned with compassion for her son; and she said, "O my Lord, give her the living child, and by no means kill him!" But the other said, "Let him be neither mine nor yours, but divide him." Therefore, the king answered and said, "Give the first woman the living child, and by no means kill him; she is his mother." And all of Israel heard of the judgment which the king had rendered; and they feared the king, for they saw that the wisdom of God was in him to administer justice.*

Did you notice the end of verse 28 -the wisdom of God was in Solomon to administer justice? There's proof right there that the wisdom of God is in you. Solomon needed the anointing of wisdom at the time to serve justice. You may need wisdom on a different occasion, but praise God that you have discovered that you have the power of wisdom inside you. You no longer have to wonder, "What am I going to do?" No! No! Stop that type of talk. You are anointed with the wisdom of God. You do know what to do in any situation, whether that is with your family, choosing a wife, finances, a career opportunity, an upcoming court case, getting out of debt, etc. Use what you have got. Your super power will cause you to become a superhero. I'm pretty sure the woman who received her child back regarded King Solomon as a superhero. Begin to operate in the wisdom of God. It's in you and upon you, waiting to go to work for you.

*Wisdom is the principal thing; therefore get wisdom. And in all your getting get understanding. (Proverbs 4:7)*

Before I end this section of the chapter, I'd like to look at one more anointing power out of the seven that have been invested inside you. And that power is called the anointing of might! The ability to do anything, it is a spirit that will come upon you released by God Almighty once he hears you demand it by speaking words of faith. Its job is to equip you to handle a task that you in your natural strength couldn't handle. Once again, let's go to a book full of examples of men of God just like you, who operated under this anointed power called might. The first man that I'd like to show you has a very familiar name: Samson, a man that God used mightily in his lifespan. Samson was known for his supernatural strength. He was anointed! He had the burden-removing, yoke-destroying power of God inside him. Many say that Samson's supernatural strength lay in his hair. When I first heard about that, it puzzled me, until I read about it in the word of God in Judges 16:17,

*No razor has ever come upon my head for I have been a Nazarite to God from my mother's womb. If I am shaven, then my strength will leave me, and I shall become weak, and be like any other man.*

I saw that this verse was proof that the strength that Samson had was inside him, which was the anointing. But you may say, "Wait a minute–I thought the strength he had was in his hair?" I said the same thing; that's why I was puzzled until I understood that Samson had a command to go by, which is clearly seen in Judges 16:17,

*for I have been a Nazarite to God from my mother's womb. If I am shaven, then my strength will leave me,*

It's not so much the loss of the hair that caused him to lose his strength. It was the breaking of the Nazarite command involved in the cutting of the hair. That strength, which is the anointing of might, was not in his hair. It was on the inside, and upon him when he needed it. Samson even knew who he was, that he wasn't the average man. Look back at the same scripture, Judges 16:17,

*If I am shaven, then my strength will leave me, and I shall become weak, and be like any other man.*

Son of God, are you weak like any other man? Can other men see the power of God flowing through your life? As a Christian man, are there any signs that you're anointed? Do you have any results in your life? If so, keep up the good work as you grow into the next level of the anointing. If you said, "No, that's okay," I believe we've identified why the power of God isn't working. Why? Because you don't yet know who you are. But continue to thank God for the information in this book to help you discover who you are in Christ, the anointed one and his anointing.

You have the anointing of might inside you, a spirit that will come upon you and cause you to do super heroic acts. Let's continue to look at Samson. In Judges 14:5-6,

*So Samson went down to Timnah with his father and mother, and came to the vineyards of Timnah. Now to his surprise, a young lion came roaring against him. And the spirit of the Lord came mightily upon him, and tore the lion apart as one would have torn apart a young goat, though he had nothing in his hand.*

Can a natural man truly rip a lion in half? Yes, he can! As long as God gives that man the same spirit of might that he gave Samson at that particular time, he can! When Samson had first made eye contact with the lion there was absolutely no fear! Why? Because Samson knew who he was! Samson knew that his confidence in God's anointing inside him would supercharge his natural ability, which caused him to grab the lion by his beard and just rip him in half like an already-paid phone bill.

What kind of circumstances and situations are roaring in your life? As you realize that you have the anointing of might, the power to do what you couldn't do in the natural, begin to speak by faith and say, "God, I thank you for giving me the spirit of might to overcome this problem. I am a man who knows that the spirit of might belongs to me." As you continue to do so, God will honor your faith as you rip in half the impossible and make it possible.

Now let's look at another example of Samson operating with the anointing of might upon him. Remember, the anointing is designed to remove burdens and destroy yokes. Look at Judges 15:14-16,

*When he came to Lehi, the Philistines came shouting against him. Then the spirit of the Lord came mightily upon him; and the ropes that were on his arms became like flax that is burned with fire, and his bonds broke loose from his hands. He found a fresh jawbone of a donkey, reached out his hand and took it, and killed a thousand men with it. Then Samson said, "With the jaw bone of a donkey heaps upon heaps, with the jaw bone of a donkey I have slain a thousand men!"*

I personally don't believe that even if you had an Uzi machine gun with a thousand bullets or more with a thousand men running at you, you'd be able to kill every one of them. That would be impossible in the natural. But the question I'd like you to think on is, "How in the world did one man like me and you take one jawbone of a donkey and kill a thousand men as they rushed at him to kill him?" What did you think of? Let me guess, it took the anointing of might, the ability to do anything, that gave this man this great victory. You, man of God, may be facing a thousand problems in your life: outstanding situations that seem like they'll never be solved, addictive behaviors that you're struggling with, job hassles, career problems, business situations, church issues, arguments with your wife or your teenager, whatever the case may be.  Know who you are, make up your mind right now, and say, "I know who I am! I am a man with the anointing of might. I have the ability to do what other natural men couldn't do. I am a superhero. Whatever is wrong, I can make it right because I am anointed."

Take time out, man of God, to study the other five types of the anointings that are available for you to succeed in life as you begin to find yourself dominating in every area of your life. Remember, the anointing is the fuel that causes you to go full steam ahead in your authority to dominate.

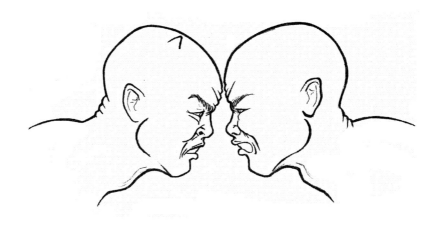

# Chapter Seven

## Super Section One: The measure vs. the tormentor

*God has dealt to each one a measure of faith. (Romans 12:3)*

Two brothers, Justin and Tavon, grew up in the big city. They also grew up in the church, where faith values and discipline in character were established. Although they grew up in the big city, neither one was subjected to gangs, drugs or fast women. Their parents, Ray and Melba, did a fine job of raising them with solid Christian values. Both Justin and Tavon had great potential. They could do just about anything they put their minds to. After graduating from high school at the top of their class, they went on to college. Justin majored in criminal justice, while Tavon majored in sports medicine.

Justin had wanted to become a FBI detective ever since he could remember. He enjoyed solving mysteries and the challenge of capturing criminals. Justin received his degree and was offered a job with his hometown police department. He accepted the job for a couple of reasons. One, he knew the streets he'd be patrolling and protecting. But he also knew he had to prove himself before becoming a detective.

Justin's brother, Tavon, also earned his degree. He wanted to help professional athletes recuperate from career-threatening injuries. He'd always enjoyed helping people. At first, Tavon wanted to become a general practitioner, but he really liked sports. He figured he could have the best of both worlds. Unlike Justin, Tavon married the woman of his dreams. They met during college. He and she decided to live where they attended college. They moved into a small two-bedroom apartment to get things started. Tavon took a job as an assistant for a sports medicine doctor. His wife, Kim, became a fifth-grade teacher at a local elementary school. Now, Tavon wanted his wife to have the very best because he loved her so. However, his credit got all screwed up after the $30,000 credit card debt he created in college. Giving his wife her dream home seemed impossible! No bank would loan Tavon any money. That didn't stop Tavon from having faith! He knew and believed God could make his dream a reality. He'd consistently tell his wife, "Baby, I am going to get you a debt-free house! Baby, I am going to get you a debt-free house! I believe God can and will do it." Tavon didn't believe the report of the world, when they told him he'd never move into a $200,000 house.

After a year in the apartment, they were nearly growing out of it. They'd acquired many possessions, including extra TVs, furniture and dishes. On top of all that, Kim was four months pregnant with their first child. Tavon was excited. He believed God would provide for his growing family. But there was a roadblock. Tavon began experiencing sharp pains in his right leg. He and his colleagues couldn't determine what was causing the pain. However, his family doctor delivered terrible news: Tavon had developed cancer in his right leg.

Tavon and Kim were devastated. But the news got worse. The doctor said Tavon had only 17 hours to live, unless he had his leg amputated. Otherwise, the doctor said the cancer could spread. Tavon had few options. However, he had to make a choice quickly.

On the other hand, after a year on the police force, Justin was doing well. His captain was very pleased with his performance. Justin stood at 6'4" and weighed about 232 pounds. He had great size for a police officer. Justin had run track and field in college. He had blazing speed. Though Justin had all the right tools to become a detective, a powerful force was holding him back. That force was fear! He often feared the possibility of dying in the line of duty. Although he was doing a great job, his negative thoughts fed the fear.

Justin worked the second shift, though he preferred the first shift. But due to seniority, he wasn't entitled to that privilege. On this particular night, Justin patrolled one of the city's toughest neighborhoods, which they called it the Red Zone. Justin was riding in his squad car, when his cell phone rang.

"How is my favorite police officer doing?"

Justin smiled, "Oh, hi, Mom. I'm doing just fine."

She said, "Good. I was just calling to let you know that I have a plate ready for you. It's your favorite: blueberry cheesecake with the graham cracker crust. I knew you'd be getting off within the next hour and I thought that you could swing by to pick it up."

Justin replied, "Yes, ma! I'll be right over as soon as I punch out."

She said, "Okay, son. I'll see you then. And always remember, son, be careful, and your daddy and I love you."

As soon as Justin hung up the cell phone, he got an emergency call from the dispatcher. Justin was ordered to go a few blocks away to answer a domestic disturbance. When Justin got to the scene, he jumped out of the car and ran to the porch. He found two little girls holding each other and crying. Justin had no time to comfort them. He saw the front door was wide open. He asked the little girls before he went into the house, "Where are mommy and daddy?"

They sobbed, "In the living room."

Justin stormed into the house. When he entered the living room, he saw the husband on top of the woman pinning her down to the floor. She looked at the officer and screamed for help. The husband had a neatly designed pottery lamp raised up in the air, ready to strike her with it.

"Stop! Freeze! This is the police!" Justin yelled.

The husband didn't listen. He broke the lamp over his wife's head. Blood went everywhere, as she screamed in pain. Although Justin could have pulled his gun and shot, he wasn't sure he could grab this man's hand, cuff him and arrest him for aggravated assault. The husband opened the window, jumped out and started running. Justin jumped out the window and began chasing him.. He ran with his gun out, not willing to shoot him, but his patience was running thin. The husband cut across a yard heading towards a fence. He knew Justin was after him. He leaped over the short fence. Justin was gaining on him and the husband knew it. When Justin hurdled the fence, the bottom of his pants leg got caught. Justin fell and hit his head. His gun fell out of his hand. He was knocked unconscious. The husband looked back and saw Justin lying on the ground and his gun lying about fifteen feet away from him. The husband ran back, picked up the gun, looked around and shot Justin twice in the chest. The husband heard police radios blaring. The husband ran, leaving Justin for dead.

Would you agree there's an enemy out there trying to steal, kill, and destroy Justin and Tavon? Let's read on.

After much prayer, Tavon and his wife, Kim, decided to have the surgery. Tavon's strength was tested, knowing he was about to lose a leg. As the nurse was preparing to wheel Tavon into the operating room, he and Kim both held hands tightly and look into each other's eyes. She whispered in his ear, "Honey, the child and I will be here by your side. I promised to be by your side, for better or for worse."

Tears streamed down his face. He said, "Thank you. I needed to hear that. The doctors say I'll never be able to walk or run again. But I have faith. I'll run and walk again and I'll get you that house. You'll see! God is still faithful and good."

Tavon's wife smiled, assured of her husband's faith. They also prayed for Justin, and Tavon asked his wife to keep tabs on Justin's health.

"I know he won't die but live, because my faith says so."

Tavon's 4 ½-hour-long surgery was successful. As the nurses rolled him out of the operating room, Kim rushed up to her husband and gave him a big kiss and hug. Tavon immediately asked, "What's going on with my brother?"

Kim gently said, "Tavon, relax. Your brother made it. Thank God, he was wearing a bulletproof vest."

With a huge sigh, Tavon simply said, "Praise God! Prayer works. It has the ability to change anything."

Meanwhile, Justin lay in his hospital bed, surrounded by fellow officers and his parents. Soon after waking up from a drug-induced sleep, he began seeing and thinking more clearly. That's when Justin's father told him about Tavon. Justin was in shock.

"No! No! Not Tavon!" he said.

"Calm down, Justin. He's doing just fine. Your father and I'll be catching the first plane out tomorrow morning to go out and be with him. Your brother's faith will sustain him," his mother said.

The captain asked Justin, "Justin, why didn't you shoot the guy after you warned him? According to the police report, you gave him a concrete warning. Anyway, the wife survived. She received sixty stitches on her head but sustained no brain damage."

Justin answered, "Sir, even though I want to be a police officer, I've never had a passion to shoot someone. But that's what my job requires. That's not to say it won't ever happen. I just choose to protect myself without killing someone. I must admit that even my heart seemed to pump as much fear as it pumps blood."

"What are you talking about?" everyone asked.

Justin confessed, "Every time I put on my uniform and head to work, I fear this could be the day I'd be shot. The thing I feared the most has happened!"

"You must not maintain that fear because, effective immediately, you are promoted to detective."

Justin was so excited he said, "My dream has come true. I'll no longer allow Satan, who came to kill, steal, and destroy, to torment me with fear.  Now I'll start using my faith as my weapon against him. I make a commitment today to meditate on what God said about fear, and he tells me in Isaiah 41:10:

*Lord is on my side, I won't fear, what can man do to me.*

"When I truly believe that the Lord is on my side, I won't fear, and besides, what can man do to me when I know God is there with me? The tormenter will no longer torment me. I'll torment him with my faith."

With less than two months to go before Kim delivers her first child, things had been going well with Tavon. He had received an artificial right leg. Determination should have been his first name. After four weeks of training with the artificial leg, surprisingly, Tavon was walking and running. Nothing could stop this man. Why? Because he knew who he was—a man of faith! A world conqueror! Jesus lived "big" inside him.

The morning after a terrible thunderstorm had blown through the town, Tavon was up and ready for his five-mile jog. He would jog from their apartment to the town's railroad station and then back—about five miles. As he was leaving, he kissed his wife's cheek and her huge stomach, which looked as though she swallowed a beach ball, carrying their unborn child. Going out the door, he turned and looked at his wife and said, "Remember, God is going to give us a debt-free home, our dream home."

Not only were they confessing and standing on God's word, they were also doing their part in the natural, making a monthly payment towards the credit card debt.

Tavon jogged down the street with his artificial leg. As people watched him run through the neighborhood on his artificial leg every day, they became inspired and realized that if you put your mind to it, you can just about accomplish anything in life.

Half a mile to the railroad tracks near the railroad station; from a distance he saw two boys and a girl rollerblading. They were having fun chasing each other. They were anywhere from nine years old to twelve years old. The kids got excited when they heard the train coming from a distance. Across from the railroad tracks was the train station. One of the boys said, "Hey let's race to the train station and the last one there has to take off their roller blades and walk all the way back home." All three agreed, including 11-year-old Emma.

"On your mark, get set, go!" All three took off racing toward the train station. From a distance, you could hear the train coming; it was blowing its horn coming into town. Emma saw that she was losing and in order to get to the train station you had to go around the end of the tracks right where the train loading dock was. Instead, she decided to get smart and cut across the train tracks. She knew that she could do it because the train was about 300 yards away. She could see and hear the train from a distance, but that didn't stop her. She wanted to win that race no matter what it took! So she skated at top speed towards the railroad tracks, but tripped over a grass-covered rock. She twisted her ankle and fell smack onto the railroad tracks. Emma screamed so loudly that all 50 states could hear her! The girl could see that the train was bearing down on her. She screamed louder and louder, "Help! Help!"

She couldn't move because her ankle was sprained. The other two boys were far ahead, focusing on winning the race. As Tavon jogged along the tracks, he heard the girl screaming for help and saw her crumpled in the middle of the track. And he saw the train racing up, so with his artificial leg, he started to run faster. He knew that he didn't have much time because the train was only about 50 yards away! As he sprinted through the grassy area to reach the girl, he also was tripping and slipping on rocks and pieces of glass from broken beer bottles. With the train only 30 yards from running over and killing the girl, Tavon speeded up even more. All of a sudden, the straps that attached his leg to him came loose, but that didn't stop him. He was determined to save this girl, his heart pounding at 200 miles per hour. He paused and pulled the strap back into place, knowing he only had seconds left. With the train only 20 yards away, he looked into the little girl's eyes and saw the terror in them. He finally reached the girl, hauled her up by her shirt collar—the horn of the train roaring at them as loud as ten thousand lions put together—then, with the girl in his arms, he leaped off the tracks with all of his might! They hit the ground and rolled into the grassy area full of rocks and broken pieces of glass. The train shot by like a rocket released from its launching pad.

Outside the café across the street, a newspaper writer had seen the whole thing transpire. He called an ambulance with his cell phone.

The next day Tavon made the front page of the newspaper; the headline read, "Man with artificial leg saves eleven-year-old child from getting run over by train." Reports of the heroic act flooded the nation.

The little girl only suffered a high ankle sprain and a few scratches. She was very thankful to the one-legged man who saved her life, and so were her parents. What Tavon didn't know was that he'd saved the life of the wealthy governor's daughter. The rich and powerful man wanted to repay Tavon. Knowing Tavon and his family lived in a small, two-bedroom apartment, he gave them a beautiful six-bedroom home, complete with spacious grounds and a built-in swimming pool. And the man's generosity didn't stop there.

The governor said, "This is only one of the tokens I'd like to give you for saving my daughter's life. Here's a $75,000 check for some pocket change. Thank you for your courage, young man."

Tavon and his wife thanked and praised God. He'd gotten a debt-free house for his wife.

Tavon said to his wife, "I didn't know God was going to give us a house with six bedrooms! He must know we're going to need them. So, after our first child, we're going to work to fill the rest of those rooms up!" "Ha, ha, ha" the young couple laughed together.

They also had enough money to pay off that credit card debt. You never know how far God will take you, if you dare to have faith in God and believe His word. God is no respecter of persons, but he is a respecter of faith! What he did for one man, he'll do for another who has faith like the first one. Have faith.

Notice that Tavon became a superhero in the eyes of a whole nation. In reality, he was a superhero on the inside first. He became a superhero on the outside by helping others. Does fear have the superhero in you in bondage? Or is faith the driving force that motivates the superhero in you? Tavon acted on the faith God gave him. How about you? Let's read on.

# Super Section Two: A factor of bondage

*Through fear of death were all their lifetime subject to bondage.*
*(Hebrews 2:15)*

"This is a man's world." We all have heard this phrase too often, or perhaps you have heard it as one of the most popular songs ever. Actually, this so-called man's world is invested with a bunch of strong men who are in bondage to a force called fear. From body builders to the shriveled-up bum on the street, from the wealthiest to the most impoverished, whether black, white, Hispanic or Asian, all have one thing in common. They all are in bondage to the fear factor. The fact that men from all walks of life are tormented with the spirit of fear is unbelievable. If you are really honest with yourself, you may realize that deep down inside your spirit man, which is your heart, is a pair of vice grips that are tightly fastened around your unstable spirit. When a man does not know who he really is in Christ, he is subject to the bondage o r vice grips of fear. A large number of men tend to hide behind the factor of fear. They put on a macho mask to look like something they are not. Many men even fear to seek help by telling someone that they are in bondage to fear. Can you see that the root of a prideful man is fear? "I'm too good to ask for help in this area of my life– asking for help will make me look weak or helpless!" The Bible says that pride comes before destruction, so you could say that a man who tolerates fear will live a life of devastating destruction.

Men that are angry, men that are addicted to drugs, sex, or alcohol, men who beat on women or a man that beats up his wife—these are men who are rooted and grounded in fear!

Men who cheat, lie, steal, and commit murders are in bondage to fear. Men who molest children, rape women and even commit suicide are men who are motivated by fear.

I know for a fact that men do such things because of the force of fear. While I was in prison, I asked some of the inmates, "Why did you really do this or that", and they'd say, "Because I feared that this would happen to me so I did this or that." Please, man of God, what I'm about to share with you is vital information for you or someone you may know who struggles with the spirit of fear.        You may honestly ask, "What is fear?" There isn't anything wrong with that question. Why? Because most men, including you, could be doing something generated by fear and not even know it!

Fear is a tormenter; it has the ability to torment you. Satan is the author behind this tormenting spirit called fear. Satan torments men by injecting evil thoughts into the mind. Thoughts such as, "You'll never ever make it! You are a big failure. God does not care about you. Go ahead and smoke some more crack–it will make you feel better. Go ahead and have some more sex–after all, it could be your last chance before you die. Give up! Stop dreaming! You don't qualify for that job. She's cheating on you. You're stupid to be with her! No one likes you. You're not good enough, etc."

These thoughts from Satan cause a man to do things that he really didn't want to do but because of the force behind the fear, he ends up living a tormented lifestyle.

There was a man in the Bible that everyone has talked about. They say religiously that this man was patient. He was a man of endurance. He endured to the end. God really tested him! His name was Job. He was the richest man in the east, and the Bible says that he was an upright man. However, although Job was rich and was an upright man before God, the force of fear tormented him. I remember before I had a better understanding of the word of God that I made such religious statements such as, "Job was patient and God was testing Job, and so on." But after getting a different understanding from my spiritual father, Creflo Dollar, I now see exactly what was really going on with Job. Job didn't know who he really was! And as you know, when you don't know who you really are in Christ, torment is there.

Fear is the opposite of faith, just like cold is the opposite of hot. Faith comes by hearing the word of God, while fear comes by hearing the words of the devil. Faith is the powerful force God uses to form and create. Fear is the powerful force that steals, kills and destroys.

As I mentioned earlier, we as men must get into the presence of God, which is his word, and look at the men of God as our example. Some are good examples, some are bad but, bad or good, God wants us to learn something from each character so we'll be able to strengthen our walk with God as well as our Christian lifestyle.

Let's look at the word of God and read about Job, and see if he was just a patient man that God was testing or if he was simply a man who operated in fear. Look at Job 1:5,

*So it was, when the days of feasting had run their course that Job would send and sanctify them. And he'd rise early in the morning and offer burnt offerings according to the number of them all. For Job said, "It may be that my sons have sinned and cursed God in their hearts." Thus Job did regularly.*

Here's Job going to God every morning and basically praying a prayer of fear! You may say, how? After all, he was praying to God not to let anything bad happen to his children because he thought that they were going to curse God. Did God respond to Job's prayer? Of course not! Why? Because he was praying and giving burnt offerings out of fear instead of faith. Well, what is a faith prayer, you may ask? It is a prayer that is prayed out of faith. Faith is the word of God. So, if faith is the word of God, pray the word! Job could have prayed, "Dear Father, I ask you to protect my children while they are out in the world doing their thing. You told me in your word to trust you at all times. And I send these burnt offerings up to you in faith, not in fear. I am trusting in you, Amen." But he didn't, and as we go along you'll see why. Now look at Job 1:11-12,

*"But now, stretch out your hand and touch all that he has, and he'll surely Curse you to your face!" And the Lord said to Satan, "Behold, all that he has is in your power; only don't lay a hand on him."*

Satan is contending for Job's life and everything he owns. After Satan had mentioned in other words to take Job out, I can imagine what God had said back to Satan. Look at verse 12 again—God then told Satan, "Behold, all that he has is in your power; you stupid dummy!!!"

God was trying to get the devil to see the fact that everything that Job has including his children are already in your hands. Why? Because Job was tormented by fear! How do we know that this is true? Go to Job 2:18,

*Another also came and said, "Your sons and daughters were eating and drinking wine in their oldest brother's house, and suddenly a great wind came from across the wilderness and struck the four corners of the house, and it fell on the young people, and they are dead; and I alone have escaped to tell you!"*

Now you see that Job's children are dead! Let's go on to look at Job 3:25 ,

*For the thing, I greatly feared has come upon me, and what I dreaded has happened to me.*

I think you now have a better understanding why Job lost all that he had, including his children. Can you see where religious, old traditions have us thinking that God was testing Job by taking everything away from him? Question, did God kill Job's sons and daughters, or was it Job's fear that caused him to lose his sons and daughters? I know you guessed right. It was Job's fear that tormented him on a daily basis. Think about this next question. What is it in your life that's tormenting you?

If fear is tormenting you with something, I suggest that you get into the word of God and find out what God said about fear. If you don't, it will only be a result of you saying, just like Job did, "The thing that I feared the most has come upon me."

Fear is so tormenting that it will bring to pass whatever you fear. Fear is a law; it will work for anyone who gets involved with it. If the speed limit is 45 mph and you are doing 65 mph, you are breaking the law! The result will be a ticket for breaking the law. I was tormented by an abusive stepfather, who both verbally and physically abused me. I was told that I wasn't going to amount to anything. I was told that I was too dumb and slow. I was told to give up my dreams, go and work in some factory for the rest of my life. As I went on to high school, others would laugh at me because I just didn't fit in. I had a girlfriend who cheated on me all of the time. My mom and stepdad got a divorce after years of marriage, and shortly afterwards my stepdad married my mom's best friend and moved into my mom's dream home. That devastated my mom as well as me. All that I went through created a serious root in the ground of my heart and that root was insecurity. That thing was a monster! You see, insecurity is a tormenter. And the root of insecurity is fear!

So I walked around for years being tormented by fear in my insecurity. Relationships that I was involved in were destroyed because I feared that the woman I was with would cheat on me like the other women did. And what could have become awesome relationships were blocked by a tormenting fear. Sometimes I'd walk into a room and wonder whether people were talking about me–about my suit, my shoes, my haircut, or maybe they were repeating something bad about me. But after I had experienced those negative thoughts, I'd feel so stupid! Why? Because those same people would come up to me and said, "Hey, Keith when you first walked through the door everyone noticed how fine you looked in that suit."

Can you see the root to those negative, false thoughts that I was having? You're right, it was fear! Fear tormented my thought life. Is fear of what people say or think about you in a negative way tormenting you? If so, please hurry and get yourself free from that people bondage! That's one of the worst bondages there is. You may say, "Yes, how do I destroy that tormenting bondage?" Easy! By destroying the root to being in people bondage, which is fear. Open the word of God and find out who you are! You are a child of God! Be yourself. Decide to care less about what people think about you. Keep in mind that people will always talk about you. If you're a millionaire or a "poorinaire," whether you're ugly or you look good, fat or skinny, white or black, that's just the way it is. You are a strong man of God! No matter how bad your past was, just know in your heart that God has forgiven you. You are about to locate God's will for your life. That will give you a fear-free life.

The law of fear has the capability to connect you to whatever you fear. Job is a perfect example. Faith will bring to pass whatever you believe God for, just like fear will bring to pass whatever you fear. You probably could write out a long list of all the terrible things that happened to you in your life. Now if you can remember, ask yourself, "Before that terrible thing happened, what did I fear, or did I fear that this was going to happen to me before it happened?"

If you fear losing your job, you'll lose your job. If you fear losing your wife or a girlfriend who has the potential to be a loving wife to you, you'll lose her. If you fear that someone will rob you, that fear will connect you to someone robbing you. If you fear that you'll lose your home in a hurricane or some blizzard, snowstorm, the fear of that storm will connect you to losing your home. If you fear being in poverty for the rest of your life, that fear will connect you to failure. God didn't put Job 3:25 in the Bible just for decoration! He put it in there for your learning, for you to know that Satan has a law called fear, and that if any man gets involved with that law it will work on him. I can say, Amen, to that because that law has been operating in my life so many times, not because of the law itself but because I yielded to the law of fear.

Now let me give a general outlook on how fear works. In order for fear to work, it needs your cooperation. Once a man gives in to fear, the force behind the fear will push you into Satan's desired results. Here's a perfect illustration.

I was once in a relationship with a woman that I cared a whole lot about and she felt the same for me. The relationship was going well, growing, and had a tremendous amount of potential to be something special, but that didn't last long. Why? Because of the past relationships that I had been in that were full of pain and hurt. Out of all that pain and hurt, my insecurity was formed. We learned earlier that fear is the headquarters to insecurity. So now, here's a woman in my life who is treating me like a king, and fear knocks on my door and says, "This is too good to be true. Now you know that this isn't real. She is going to hurt you just like the rest of the women you had." The torment of fear would then say to me, "Who do you think you are? You're not good enough for her! You don't have anything to offer her! Look at your muscles; they are not big like so and so's! Look at the car you drive. It's all broken down and rusted out! It won't be long before she finds another guy who has bigger muscles than you and drives a better car than you." Now once I paid attention to the voice of fear, which is Satan, the force of fear began to move me to accuse this woman of looking at every man that was in the same area we were in such as restaurants, malls, grocery stores, and even at church! I'd say things like, "Why are you looking at that guy? Is it because he has big muscles or a better car than me?" And she'd say, "No! I'm not looking at anyone except you. I like your muscles. I like your car. Not theirs!" That was too hard for me to believe. The grip of fear forced me to believe otherwise. So, I continued being tormented by the fear of her leaving me. That fear eventually made my thought become a reality. What I feared the most came true–she left me.

You have learned that fear will connect you to whatever you fear. Now we must identify the forces that generate the spirit of fear. If you can honestly say that you are a man of fear, take time to locate the evil forces that are coming from fear. Your evil force could be anger, worry, low self-esteem, selfishness, pride, anxiety, envy, or jealousy. A man is jealous because he fears that he cannot obtain what someone else has obtained. But all he has to do is find out what God has called him to do and what God has for him. Begin now to locate the evil forces that are causing you to fear.

# Super Section Three: Paralyzed from succeeding

*...men's hearts failing them from fear. (Luke 21:26)*

Listen, man of God, if you don't deal with the spirit of fear, it will not only torment you, it will paralyze you from being successful in your life. God has called you to be a superhero–a man who succeeds at anything. Could it be that you failed to unwrap your package of success because you are paralyzed by fear?

God has given us a command we see all through the Bible: Fear not! Fear not! Fear not! Why would God say this so often in the Bible? Because you and I are men of faith! And whatever God has called you to do, it's going require you to be fearless. His ultimate desire is to see his sons, you and I, succeeding in this corrupted world.

Men's hearts are failing them because of the spirit of fear. What does it actually mean when the Bible says that men's hearts fail them because of fear? My interpretation would be that men are living a life of failure because the root of fear is deep in their hearts. But there is so much power invested inside you that fear should have no room to linger in your heart. As you have read in the previous chapter, you are the righteousness of God, you are a man that has been created to dominate on this earth, you are a man who is possessed with the same authority that Jesus had when he walked on this earth! You are a covenant man with God, you have rights that you can tap into so you can live like a king in the eyes of others. You are a powerful, powerful man! Young or old, it does not matter. The superhero is inside of you ready to explode here on the earth.

Failure to exercise and tap into the powers that were just mentioned, failure to understand how they operate, is a huge failure that erupts out of a heart full of fear. Men, the spirit of fear is real. Fear will stop you from experiencing God's best for your life. You may be in need for a miracle but it won't manifest in your life because of fear. Thousands upon thousands die every day, young and old, on a hospital bed because of the spirit of fear, when they had plenty of time left to live on this earth. Thousands upon thousands flood the courtrooms and have years of their life taken away from them because of crime that they committed out of fear. I wonder how many men, including you, have the potential to be someone great, but the spirit of fear says to you, "No! You cannot do that. It will never work out. You are just dreaming–get real. Look at you, how could you be that or do that when right now you are a nobody? You're too small, too big, too dumb, too skinny, too fat, no experience, no education, no nothing." This is the language of fear. It is often true that you pay more attention to this language than you do the language of faith!

If you said, "Okay, that's me; I am a man of fear," that's okay for now. I appreciate your honesty. After reading this chapter, you'll get out from underneath the weight of fear. But first, I must show you that you are not alone in living a life of fear. I want to show you in the word of God men that were paralyzed by the spirit of fear. Look with me at Matthew 14:25,

*Now in the fourth watch of the night Jesus went to them, walking on the sea. And when the disciples saw him walking on the sea, they were troubled, saying, "It is a ghost!" and they cried out for fear. But immediately Jesus spoke to them, saying, "Be of good cheer! It is I; don't be afraid." And Peter answered him and said, "Lord if it is you, command me to come to you on the water." So he said, "Come," and when Peter had come down out of the boat he walked on water to go to Jesus. But when he saw that the wind was boisterous, he was afraid; and beginning to sink he cried out, saying, "Lord, save me!" And immediately Jesus stretched out his hand and caught him, and said to him, "O you of little faith, why did you doubt?" And when they got into the boat, the wind ceased.*

This is the Apostle Peter, a strong man of faith! In fact, he was closer to Jesus than any other disciple that Jesus had. Peter was a man of faith who wrote two books in the Bible, whose shadow healed people when he walked by them, who laid hands on the sick and they recovered, who preached the Gospel of Jesus Christ with boldness and authority. Watch this! Peter walked on water! I tell people often that you can say what you want about Peter, but the man walked on water!!! When was the last time you saw a man walk on water?

Even though Peter walked on the water, after a few more steps he began to sink! Why?

1. He took his eyes off Jesus.
2. He then began to look at the boisterous winds.
3. And he was afraid.
4. His fear connected him to what he was afraid of–sinking.

These are the four steps that caused Peter to sink. But as he put these four steps into motion, what did Peter open the door to? Fear!

As Peter began to walk across the water, he had a short burst of faith but soon was paralyzed by fear which caused him to take his eyes of

Jesus, look at the wild winds, and sink down into the waves.

When you look to Jesus by looking into the word of God, and begin to find out who you are in Christ and learn of his ways of life, you'll begin to live an abundant, peaceful, joyful, prosperous, and successful lifestyle. But when you take your eyes and your attention off Jesus, you'll suffer the pain of paralyzed living, a stressful life, worry, insecurities, anger, poverty and everything else subject under the curse of the law of sin and death. The cause of this law going into effect—"the spirit of fear."

No wonder you have not had the opportunity to enjoy the good life! Opportunity meets preparation. But you were preparing yourself in fear, by practicing being fearful, so when the opportunity knocked on your door, you were paralyzed by fear and couldn't respond for success.

I am qualified to write about fear. Why? Because fear had me paralyzed in every area of my life. When I played two years of semi-pro football in Chicago and came into training camp as the fastest starting free safety on the team, the coaches were very impressed with my work ethic and my attitude to win! But as soon as I touched the field to play ball, I was tormented by fear. I could hear the enemy say to me, "You are going to break your neck if you try to make that tackle," or, "you are going to drop the ball if you try to intercept it!" Well, after receiving those negative thoughts and words, I immediately became paralyzed on the field. Running backs, full backs, and wide receivers would just blow right pass me! Throughout the game, interceptions would present themselves to me. I'd make some effort to jump up in the air, catch the ball, go back the other way, and score a touchdown. But it never happened. Why? Because when I did jump into the air, I'd drop the football instead of catch it. And I'd say that the thing that I feared the most has come upon me. By the third game of the season, I'd find myself on the bench not able to participate in any of the remaining games. Now that I have identified the problem that stopped my success, I've discovered that I'll no longer be paralyzed by fear but will be energized by faith!

Remember to evaluate yourself. This is serious, man. Fear is or could be keeping the superhero asleep inside you. Ask yourself what is it that I always wanted to do in life but I am paralyzed to do it?

That's a good question to ask, I often ask myself that question. And this same question reminds me of the story about the rich, young ruler. Here's a guy who was completely paralyzed by the spirit of fear. Look with me at Luke 18:18-22 ,

*Now a certain ruler asked him, saying, "Good teacher, what shall I do to inherit eternal life?" So Jesus said to him, "Why do you call me good? No one is good but One, that is, God. You know the commandments: Don't commit adultery, don't murder, don't steal and don't bear false witness, honor your father and your mother." And he said, "All these things I have kept from my youth." So when Jesus heard these things, he said to him, "You still lack one thing. Sell all that you have and distribute to the poor, and you'll have treasure in heaven; and come, follow me."*

I'm pretty sure that this rich young man had known about Jesus all of his life, and he knew that Jesus had the key to what he desired the most: how to inherit eternal life. Well, he finally had his chance to meet with Jesus and asked him, "How can I inherit eternal life?"

Jesus responded, "You can inherit eternal life by starting out keeping God's commandments."

The rich young ruler then said, "I have kept all of God's commandments to the best of my ability."

Man of God, here's one way to get rich–keep God's commandments. You cannot keep the commandments of God and *not* prosper in life. Jesus then said, "True, you have kept the commandments, but you do lack one."

The young man then said, "Which one?"

Jesus then said, "Go and sell all that you have and give all of your money to the poor. And come and follow me, so that you can receive eternal life."

But the rich young ruler became very sorrowful and was "paralyzed." He couldn't even take a step. Why? Because the spirit of fear had snatched his heart, which had a dream to inherit eternal life. The opportunity was knocking at the door of his heart; he had the chance not to just inherit eternal life but also to follow Jesus. Had he obeyed that one commandment, the commandment of love to give all that he had, which is an act of love. He'd have received double what he gave away; but he missed that opportunity because of fear. Although he kept the most of the commandments, he actually couldn't keep the others. He put riches before God. He didn't want to lose everything, so fear paralyzed him. A man whose heart was full of himself and riches with no room for Jesus Christ, the anointed one, and his anointing–it would be hard for him to make it into heaven. But the man who has the anointed one in his heart ,and is willing to share the love of God to others and not be tormented by fear–that's the man who won't only make it into heaven but he'll have heaven on earth.

Man of God, God didn't give you the spirit of fear, so the next time you begin to fear, say, "No! I am going to face this fear because fear didn't come from God and God is in me! I am a superhero in this situation and superheroes don't fear! They boldly face their fears and have victory over them."

You are more than a conqueror. How do I know? Because the word says so. Look at Romans 8:37,

*Yet, in all these things we are more than conquerors through him who loved us.*

The word of God says you are more than conquerors, which tells you that you can conquer fear! Look what else it tells you about fear in Isaiah 41:10,

*Fear not, there's nothing to fear, for I am with you.*

When you know in your heart that God is with you everywhere you go, in all that you do, there will not be any fear! Because you know that God is with you! He is with you on your job. He is with you in your career. He is with you in the important business meeting. He is with you in your marriage. He is with you in the prison. He is with you while you are waiting in the hospital. He is with you at school. He's in the courtroom with you. Right now while you are standing in the circle of problems or cannot seem to see your way out of your life storms, you'll soar out of them all if you only do your part. And your part is NOT to fear because there's nothing *to* fear, for God is with you!
You may say, "Wait a minute–you don't understand. I am a police officer (or, I am in the military or, I am a taxi cab driver), yet I do my job well. I still receive threats on my life!" Justin who was a police officer also dealt with fear, and you saw what happened to him. The result, the thing he feared the most had come upon him. But that doesn't have to happen to you! Why? Because of what Psalm 118:6 says,

*The Lord is on my side; I won't fear. What can man do to me?*

No matter what you do in life, when you have to deal with all kinds of mindsets of people, you don't have to fear, because you know that the Lord is on your side, so what can a man do to you? Once you get that in your heart, fear of people will no longer exist in you.
Fear not! Fear not! Fear not! Go back and get what the enemy has stolen from you when he used you to yield to the spirit of fear. The enemy has to restore back to you sevenfold what you lost. The enemy is fear himself, and he is terribly afraid of you. Why? Because he knows that once you discover who you really are in Christ, he won't have any control over you anymore–he knows that you'll have control over him!
If you have discovered that fear has tormented you and paralyzed you, pick those broken dreams back up , step back out on that opportunity to become a business owner, go back and retrieve the wife and children you left behind. Whatever it may be–you know what you have lost! And now you are equipped to overcome fear with your super power of facing your fear. Remember this true statement: Christ has already redeemed, delivered you from the curse of the law of sin and death. And as you know, fear is under that law. You are in Christ; he already paid the price to free you from fear. Receive your freedom and use your faith as Tavon did. He's your example of a fearless man who lets the superhero go free. Fear not and let him go. Who is "him"? The "him"

is you, the superhero.

# Super Section Four: You are a man of faith

*The just shall live by faith. (Galatians 3:11)*

You are the just, which means the day you made Jesus Lord over your life, you became justified as a son of God; you became justified as the righteousness of God; you became justified as an heir, a partaker of Jesus Christ, the anointed one and his anointing. In order to know that you are justified, you have to believe and receive that you have been justified.

The root of the word justified is the word "just." The above scripture says that the just shall live by faith, and you are the just, which qualifies you to live by faith. Far too many Christian men have lived a life of condemnation, which is rooted in fear. A very small percentage of Christian men are living a life of justification, which is rooted in faith. That percentage, my friend, has to change, it will change, and that change will have to start with you! You are a man of faith! That's exactly who you are! After reading this section of this chapter, you'll know what the opposite of fear is, which is faith, and live a lifestyle of faith. There are men who truly desire to live a life of faith but they don't know how. They or you may have heard religious phrases such as, "You gotta have faith as small as a mustard seed! Just have faith everything is going to be okay. See, it didn't work for you because you didn't have enough faith!" And I am not saying these statements are wrong, I just understand that they are incomplete, like a dropped pass thrown by a quarterback. That's what religion is: something that you do or say that's not born out of the heart. Jesus said in Matthew 15:8-9,

*These people draw near to me with their mouth, and honor me with their lips, but their heart is far from me.*

I have often heard men say, "I don't have any faith," or, "I am going to pray more so that I can get some more faith." Such statements come from a lack of understanding. I remember when I thought the same thing. What a frustrating feeling.

As you have already seen at the beginning of the chapter, God has given every man a measure of faith (Romans 12:3). You, man of God, no longer have to live in frustration about whether you have faith or not. God has given you a measure of faith. The day you became born again a measure of faith seed was sown into the ground of your heart, like a farmer sows a corn seed into the ground of his field. You were born out of your mother's womb with a very small bicep. As you got older that muscle began to grow a little and perhaps one day you wanted to develop your bicep muscle into a bigger, harder, stronger bicep. But to do so, you had to exercise that particular muscle with pressure by using heavy weight equipment. Although at first you couldn't see progress of that muscle getting bigger, it really was growing. But you must continue to exercise that muscle in order to see results.

Likewise, this is how your faith works; you no longer have to pray for more faith–you already have it and God isn't going to give any more than what you already have. He has already given you all the faith that you need. Now it is up to you to develop the faith that you have inside you. A body builder didn't have to pray for more muscles the day he was born; he already had all the muscles that he was ever going to get. He simply made up in his mind to exercise his muscle and get them as big as possible. This is the type of attitude God wants us to have, one that says, I'm going to build up my faith in God just like a body builder builds his muscles. By being faithful, you'll be bigger and stronger than Mr. Universe himself!

I have asked people what faith is, since you already have it inside you, and they'd respond by saying what Hebrews 11:1 says,

*Now faith is the substance of things hoped for, the evidence of things not seen.*

Now notice what you're reading, man of God, as you are discovering who you are as a man of faith. Yes, faith is the substance of things hoped for and it is the evidence of things not seen. Faith is a spiritual force that you cannot see, just like fear is a spiritual, demonic force that you cannot see. Both will give you enormous results depending on which one you choose to live by. The spiritual force of fear will connect you to whatever you fear. And the spiritual force of faith will connect you to whatever you have faith in. That's the key behind faith results and fear results: removing the mountains in your life or causing the mountain to crush you. Remember, Satan comes to kill, steal and destroy. How? By using the spiritual force of fear, which is actually twisted faith. The Bible says in Hebrews 11:3,

*By faith, we understand that the worlds were framed by the word of God, so that the things, which are seen, were not made of things, which are visible.*

As you see in this scripture, the worlds were framed by the word of God. When God opened his mouth and said, let there be light, water, and even mankind, he spoke with faith–a spiritual force that moved the Holy Spirit to do its job. Notice in Hebrews 11:3 that by faith you and I understand the worlds were created by the word of God, which tells me that faith and the word of God are connected. Let's look at Romans 10:17,

*So then, faith comes by hearing, and hearing by the word of God.*

After reading that scripture, I confidently say that faith is the word of God. The more you read and hear the word of God, the more the measure of faith will begin to grow inside you. No word of God, no faith, no faith, no word of God. That's why it is so important, man of God, to spend some quality time in the word so that you can build up your faith.

As you get into the word of God, begin to locate what you need in life. If you need healing, find out what the word of God says about healing. If you need deliverance, look into the word and find out what it says about deliverance. If you need finances, open the word of God and find out what it has to say concerning finances. If you are looking for a complete change of life, pick up your Bible and do some investigation on how to change.

You see, men of God, answers are in the presence of God and when you are in his word, you are in the presence of God, because God is his word speaking directly to you. Some failures in life develop because of a failure to get into the word of God. Now, I wrote all of that to set you up for a law that you must obey if you are ever going to see your faith work for you. As you know now, faith is the word of God and the word of God is faith. In other important words, faith is acting on the word of God. This law that I'm about to explain is called the law of faith. The law of faith will work for you just like the law of seed, time and harvest will work for you. If you sow good seeds, you'll receive a good harvest. If you sow bad seeds, you'll receive a bad harvest. That's just the way it is-it's a law! Now let's read how the law of faith works. Look with me at Mark 11:23-26 ,

*For assuredly, I say to you, whoever says to this mountain, "Be removed and cast into the sea," and does not doubt in his heart, but believes that those things he says will be done, he'll have whatever he says. Therefore I say unto you , whatever things you ask when you pray, believe that you receive them, and you'll have them. And whenever you stand praying, if you have anything against anyone, forgive him, that your father in heaven may also forgive you your trespasses. But if you don't forgive, neither will your father in heaven forgive your trespasses.*

When you operate under the law of faith you have the ability to have whatsoever you say. Now that's an awesome ability! You have the power to have whatever you say out of your mouth. According to verse 23, the first rule of the law of faith is:

Faith speaks and it says to this mountain, be removed and be cast into the sea. Here is Jesus giving you an order to speak or say to the mountains of your life. He didn't say go around the mountains, nor did he say go and get worldly advice, help and opinions to get rid of the mountains in your life. No! He said you use your faith by speaking the word of God on the tasks that you are facing. You, man of God, determine the outcome of your life by the words that you speak or say out of your mouth. The Bible says in Proverbs 18:21, "Life and death are in the power of the tongue." See, you have another power inside you, your tongue! It has the ability to create life or death. Begin to use your super heroic power by speaking positive confessions over your life so that you can have a positive and fulfilled lifestyle.

Never doubt. Also in verse 23 it says, "...does not doubt in his heart, but believes that those things which he says will be done, he'll have whatever he says." If belief were a person, his home would be the heart. But if doubt were a person, he'd have the ability to evict belief out of the heart. Doubt has power! This is why it's a rule, because of its destroying power over a believing faith heart. If there is doubt in your heart, begin to fill the three gateways to the heart with the word of God:

- looking at the word of God,
- speaking and confessing the word of God, and
- hearing and listening to the word of God.


Look at the promises of God; this will produce belief in your heart. Speak the promises of God over and over again over your life. Hear the word of God on a continuous basis. By doing those three steps, your heart will be filled with faith and all doubt will be washed out. What you give the most attention to, that's what will get into your heart.

Receive what you are believing. How would it make you feel if you were to give me a special gift and I didn't want to receive your gift? It wouldn't feel right at all! That's how God feels when you by faith don't receive the promises that he has made available for you. In verse 24 it says, "Therefore I say to you, whatever things you ask when you pray, believe that you receive them and you'll have them." Here's another rule to the law of faith: you are going to not only believe but you are going to have to receive by faith right now! Whenever you ask God for something, believe it and receive it right then and there. Act as though you already have it! When you do, so you are now fulfilling a rule of the law of faith.

Forgive, forgive, forgive! One of the reasons you have not experienced the power of faith in your life is because of unforgiveness. That is a major spirit that will absolutely rob you of walking by faith and receiving God's best! Being an unforgiving man is definitely not who you are! You are a man of God, a Son of God, and a child of God! So since God is inside of you and he is a merciful and forgiving God, why can you not be a merciful and forgiving man of God? This is a rule of the law of faith: you must forgive. Why not start right now! Why? Because your faith is on the line when you don't do so.

This is the law of faith, so begin to understand the law of faith and practice it. What can you do or how effective can you be without understanding? Faith is in you, in fact in Romans 10:8 it states,

*The word is near you, in your mouth and in your heart.*

God spoke words out of his mouth, words that were so powerful that they created and framed the universe, including you and me! Question, what propelled those words out of his mouth? My friend, it was the spiritual force of faith! Faith is the word acted upon and that word is in you like it was in God, for it is also located in the heart of a man. I'll never ever forget Pastor Taffi L. Dollar saying, "If you are not saying anything, you are not creating anything." What a powerful statement. Can you see the power that God has given you when you speak words from a believing heart instead of a heart full of fear?

Walking in faith is your justice and if you are in trouble, no matter what the case may be, begin to use what faith you have! After all, you have been given an order by God, and that order is the simple fact, the just shall live by faith.

# Super Section Five: You are going to have to do your part

*However, without faith it is impossible to please him. (Hebrews 11:6)*

As you already know, faith, which is the word of God acted upon, will work for you. And you also remember that if you don't have any word you won't have any faith. And if you don't have any faith that would be an indication that you don't have any word! Although you had faith when you gave your life to Christ, if you don't exercise that faith, it will never grow to be explosive in your life and the lives of others.

God requires you to live a life of faith instead of fear. Faith, I believe, is one of the most important subjects in the Bible for any man to learn, whether he just got born again or has been saved for the last ten years. The love of God and walking as a man of Love is the most important subject in the Bible. It does not matter if you have mountain-moving faith—if it isn't supported by the love of God, your faith will just be powerless! And if you have been exercising your faith and it has not been effective in producing results, this would be one main area in your life that you'd need to check. Even though you are exercising your muscles with intense pressure by using heavy equipment such as weights, if you don't intake the substance of protein which supports the muscle to grow, chances are your muscle won't fully develop. Likewise, if you fail to walk in love with others and God, your faith will also be a major failure. Look at Galatians 5:6,

*Faith worketh by love.*

Later in this book, we'll discuss the most powerful force on this planet which is also already inside you.

Walking in faith is the duty of a man of God. In fact, if you're ever going to see a miracle, debt cancellation, prosperity, healing, a dream fulfilled, a promotion, a godly and virtuous wife, restoration in a marriage, or whatever your heart desires, it's going to require faith! Whatever it is in your heart that you desire can become a reality if you'd use what you have inside you and in life. You see, your desires and dreams must line up with the word of God. If you need money, go to the word of God and find out God's way to get the money you need. For example, you need $500 more to pay on a certain bill and you have less than 24 hours to pay for it. At this point, you don't know what to do and you are faced with the decision of operating in the requirement of faith or the enemy's requirement of fear. But you choose to operate under the requirement of faith. So, you pick up your Bible and learn what you need to do to pay off a bill, and while you are searching the scriptures you run across Matthew 6:33 ,

*But seek first the kingdom of God and his righteousness, and all these things will be added to you.*

So now you find the word of God that you can act upon–by going out seeking the kingdom of God. How? Giving to the poor or someone in need, soul-winning, getting involved in projects that are trying to build up the kingdom of God, while knowing He will provide, will bring the money you need. That's how faith works! Just act on the word of God–whatever it says for you to do, do it! If it says give, give! If it says forgive, forgive! If it says seek the kingdom of God, seek the kingdom of God. Speaking of Matthew 6:33, ask yourself these questions, "Have my needs been met? Have all the things that I have ever dreamed of shown up yet in my life?" Perhaps, you haven't been doing your part, which is seeking the kingdom of God. Always remember when you're reading God's precious promises, begin to look at what your part is. If you'll begin to do your part, God will definitely do his part! Could it be, man of God, you have not experienced the fullness of God's promises happening in your life because you failed to act on them—which is faith?

You see, man of God, one of the ways to please God is to walk by and live by faith. We all want to please God, and here's one way to do so. Practice operating in the power that you have, which is your faith. Superheroes are successful because they don't neglect their faith; they always face their fears and attack the enemy by using the power of faith! If you read the whole eleventh chapter of Hebrews, you'll find a number of men who operated in faith. These were men who knew who they were, and they all had close relationships with God. Noah, Abraham, Joseph and Moses were considered superheroes of old. How? They used their faith. Hebrews 11:32-35 says,

*And what more shall I say? For the time would fail me to tell of Gideon and Barak and Samson and Jephthah, also of David and Samuel and the prophets: who through faith subdued kingdoms, worked righteousness, obtained promises, stopped the mouths of lions, quenched the violence of fire, escaped the edge of the sword, out of weakness were made strong, became valiant in battle, turned to flight the armies of the aliens. Woman received their dead raised to life again.*

Now these superheroes of faith didn't have a Bible to read and meditate on like you and I have. You may ask, "Well, how did they operate in faith if they didn't have the source to get the faith, which is the Bible?" Good question, and here's a good, valid answer; they had the voice of God. God specifically spoke to their hearts and told them to do this or that and they did what was asked of them! Now that was faith, how? They acted on God's spoken word. You and I have his written word and his spoken word. To have a successful life of faith you must understand the difference between the written word and God's spoken word. For example, God's word says in Mark 16:15,

*Go ye into the world and preach the gospel.*

That is what God has commissioned all of us to do in whatever arena of life in which we dwell. Even though we've been commanded to preach the good news, we must tune into hear God's spoken voice, which may say, "I know you are excited to go to Africa to preach the gospel but I need you in Japan to preach the gospel there. It's not the time for Africa yet." The key is to find out exactly where God wants you to go, for his written word just says go into the world and preach the gospel. Well, you may ask, "What if I don't hear God's voice behind his written word?" Then just obey the written word. You see, whenever you find yourself obeying and doing what is written by God, plus what you hear spoken to you by God himself, you'll be walking and living by faith. Can you now see the advantage you have over the superheroes of old?

You have the written word *and* God's spoken word to help you live by faith. You have all of this power inside and sitting on your lap during church service on Bible study night or on Sunday mornings. Failure to act on the written word or the spoken word will only lead you down a dark tunnel of disappointment.

One of the main objectives in this chapter is to get you to understand who you really are (a man of faith) by knowing the importance of you doing your part to make the God kind of faith work for you.

God has already done his part by getting faith to us. How did he do that? He did it by the death and the resurrection of his only begotten son, Jesus Christ. As you may or may not know, Jesus died for you and me. Through his death, he redeemed (delivered) you from the curse of the law. Look at Galatians 3:13-14,

*Christ has redeemed (delivered) us from the curse of the law, having become a curse for us (for it is written, "Cursed is everyone who hangs on a tree"), that the blessing of Abraham might come upon the Gentiles in Christ Jesus, that we might receive the promise of the Spirit through faith.*

Under the curse of the law lies:

- Sickness and disease
- Poverty
- Debt
- Death (the sting of death)
- Fear
- People bondage
- Drug and sexual addictions
- Prison
- Internal addictions such as anger, pride, male chauvinist attitudes, etc.

All of these are curses that a man of God should not be living under. If you are currently being controlled by anything that is stopping you from prospering mentally, spiritually and physically as a man of God, something is wrong! And the problem is–you don't know who you are in Christ Jesus. When you received Jesus Christ as Lord and Savior over your life, you received deliverance from the curse.

I remember this revelation hitting me smack in my heart. I said to myself, "If Jesus had died for me and has already delivered me from the curse of the law of sin and death, why am I still sick? Why am I still broke? Why am I still addicted to masturbation? Why do I fear? Why can I not have successful relationships with friends, family members and potential wife material?" And one of the most vital answers to all my "whys" was: I just didn't know who I was in Christ even though I went to church every time the doors opened, even though I spent a year with Creflo Dollar as he mentored me to change. I paid attention and learned a lot but that does not amount to anything if you are not willing to apply or practice, and that's something I didn't do. I finally realized that Jesus took my infirmities and sicknesses that I may be healed. Jesus became poor that I may become rich! When I accepted him I became a Son of God and no longer a slave to the world. The same is true for you, Son of God. You may say, "Okay, that makes sense, it is the word of God–but how can I obtain those promises that are available for me?" Good question, but look at Galatians 3:14 again, especially the last part of verse 14,

*That we might receive the promise of the spirit through faith.*

Did you catch the answer to why you may not have broken the chains of the curse over your life? That's right; it's going to require faith! All of the promises in the Bible are guaranteed to you if you'll act on the word of God. If Jesus has told you in the word of God that he has redeemed (delivered) you from the curse of the law of sin and death, just make a quality decision to act like it is so. Just "man up" and say, "I am a man of God. I don't have to stay in bondage to this or that. I am a Son of God and through Jesus Christ, I no longer have to be in lack and live a life of poverty. I have been adopted into the family of God and in his family there is no sickness or disease. I am healed right now!" Continue to say that repeatedly. Begin to have a new walk about yourself, a new look and a new attitude knowing what God is about to do for you in your life. Keep in mind you must act on whatever you read in the word of God. That, my friend, is what you call faith!

Notice I told you to continue to repeat what you say you want to happen in your life. Remember that's one of the traits of the law of faith. The Bible says in Mark 11:24, "You can have what you say!" Positive or negative, Christian or sinner, this law will work for anyone. Do you remember when you were a sinner and you were at work, you kept saying, "After work I'm going to get me a beer." And you said it repeatedly until you punched out and found yourself at the nearest bar drinking a cold beer. Do you see why the Bible says, "You can have whatever you say"? If you say, "I'm going to win, I'm going to win, I'm going to win," over and over again, your words will move you to become a winner! If you say, "I'm going to lose, I'm going to lose, I'm going to lose," over and over again, your words will move you to lose. Do you see the power that you have? Take advantage of the law of faith; you can really have what you say. When you begin to confess the word of God, which is your part to do, you automatically give God permission to honor your faith.

As I end this chapter, I want to clarify a little more about what happens when you do your part as you apply and practice the law of faith. Now let's look into the mirror of life, the mirror that will allow you to see the real you, which is the word of God. God is so smart; he knew that we needed examples of people in the Bible that did their part by acting on the word of God.

Now look with me at Matthew 9:27-29,

*When Jesus departed from there, two blind men followed him, crying out and saying, "Son of David, have mercy on us!" And when he had come into the house, the blind men came to him. And Jesus said to them, "Do you believer that I am able to do this?" They said to him, "Yes, Lord." Then he touched their eyes, saying, "According to your faith let it be to you."*

Now this is an interesting short segment about two blind men that received their sight. As they heard that Jesus could heal the sick and infirmities they made their minds up to search for Jesus even though they were both blind. When a man truly makes his mind up in a thing, he becomes unstoppable! Yes, Praise God! We just read that Jesus, Almighty, touched their blinded eyes and they were opened. That's great but what you and I want to know is how did they get that particular healing to receive their sight back? They both followed Jesus, crying out, have mercy on us!

They believed that Jesus could heal their blindness. They were confident based on hearing the word of Jesus on what he could do, what he came to the earth to do, and his offer to heal them.

It was according to their faith that their eyes were healed.

What I want you to see is that it was because of the blind men's faith that they received their healing from Jesus. They did their part! They followed Jesus and kept on asking for a healing. I'm pretty sure there were people asking them to shut up and leave Jesus alone, because he was too busy for them. But small distractions didn't slow them down at all. Once they got Jesus' attention, He asked them, "Do you believe that I am able to do this?" They responded by saying, "Yes, Lord!" Jesus touched their eyes and blindness was no longer an issue is their lives. But notice what Jesus said about them on their healing, "according to your faith let it be done to you". You see, when we read about Jesus healing someone, we tend to celebrate God's manifested glory and never look at what the person did who got healed to see God's miraculous power work in his or her life. Yes! By all means, you celebrate what God has done, but also keep in mind that your part needs to be done in order to celebrate in those three steps you just read. That was their way of believing that Jesus could heal them. So they executed what they believed in and Jesus said, "According to your faith, let it be done to you." Notice not God's faith, Jesus' faith, Abraham's faith, the college coach's faith, David's faith, Joshua's faith, Joseph's faith, or your mother's faith. He said because of your faith. The blind men acted on the word of God, which is faith! These guys heard about Jesus healing others, which built their faith in him, and Jesus asked them, "Do you believe?" They acted out on those words (faith) by saying, "Yes! We believe!" They did their part.

For some reason in today's world, Christian men act as if God will come down and do something for them and when a prayer isn't answered or they don't get what they were believing God for they quickly get discouraged and ask, "Why God, why?" They do all the form stuff like talk faith, pray, and confess–which are all good to do–but the action part is left out and when there is no acting on the word of God there are no desired results. In order to get God involved in any area of your life you are going to have to give him permission to get involved in your life. How? By you first acting on his word! Once you have done that you will hear from God saying, "According to your faith, let it be to you." Keep this in mind: Whatever you're going through right now, you can come out of it a winner. That's only if you will do your part. Begin to look into the word and find the solutions to your problems. When you do so, act on them and your faith will cause you to see beyond the dark blindness of the world. Do your part, man of God.

Look with me at Matthew 9:20-22. Here's another fine example of a woman who obtained the desired promise of healing from Jesus. The question is, how did she get it? Let's read and find out what the word says,

> And, suddenly, a woman who had a flow of blood for twelve years came from behind and touched the hem of his garment. For she said to herself, "If only I may touch his garment, I shall be made well." But Jesus turned around, and when he saw her he said, "Be of good cheer, daughter; your faith has mad you well." And the woman was made well from that hour.

Now come on, men of God, men of faith, if a woman can get her heart's desire of healing, you can too. Now your heart's desire may not be healing, it may be finances, a good job opportunity, a chance to see your children again because your ex kept them away from you. Whether it's starting your own business or a new home to put your beautiful wife in–no matter what your heart's desires are they can become a reality in your life. But you must be willing to pay the price by doing your part. Well, that's what the woman with the issue of blood had to do. Her part was to act on what she had been hearing about Jesus, the miracles that he produced throughout the land. As she kept hearing about Jesus' healing ministry, her faith in what she heard began to grow and grow, then it took root in her heart. Remember, faith comes by hearing and hearing the word of God. Once she found out that Jesus was coming her way, she acted on the words that grew in her heart. After meditating over and over again on the words that Jesus can heal you, Jesus has healed this person and that person, there was no way that she was going to pass this opportunity up! She then began to put her faith into action. How? It was by pressing through a crowd of people. She also said within her heart, "If only I can touch his garment I'll be made well!" She's weaving and bumping into people. I'm pretty sure people were bumping into her as well. But that didn't stop her because she was desperate to obtain what she was believing. When you are desperate and you truly believe in something, you'll find yourself acting on what you believe! Action is believing and believing is action! Well, she finally grabbed hold of Jesus' garment and the Bible says that power left him at that point. What power? The power that was needed at that time was the power of healing. Moments later, look what Jesus said to her, "Be of good cheer, daughter. Your faith has made you well." Did you catch how this woman received her heart's desire, which was healing? It was because of her "faith," not her best friend's faith, not the disciples' faith, but her faith, gentlemen! She got what she wanted. She did her part! She got up and did something! She didn't just sit around and hope that Jesus was going to knock on her door. Instead, she had a hunting mentality–to go out and hunt Jesus down in order to get what she wanted. You as a man, and all men on this planet, have inside them the ability to hunt. God made man that way. This is why, when most men see an attractive woman, they go after her until they get their prize. Jesus has already given you and me the victory, but we must do our part to receive the stored-up victories that are available to us. I'm talking about victory in every single area of life. How can this be done? It will be done by your faith! You just consistently keep acting on God's word. It is when you do so you can be 100% sure that your faith in God's word will be manifested in your life. If you happen to be reading this in prison, you can get out! How? Change the way you think and your life will change. Pick up your Bible and find out how God thinks and then begin to think like him. You may say, "No one can think and act like God!" Oh yes, you can, because the word says in Ephesians 5:1,

*Therefore be imitators of God as dear children.*

There's your right, to imitate God instead of the world. When you imitate someone or something in the world, you don't know who you are and you'll be tormented by the spirit of fear, because of carelessly not spending time with God. You that are a prisoner have an advantage to establish a quality relationship with God. You have time to discover the real you. Once you put yourself in line with God whole-heartedly, that's when he'll, watch this, "Accept your faith" and go to moving on the parole board's heart for you. But God has to see faith coming forth from you. Yes, God and man can both see faith. Let me give you a final example. Go to Mark 2:3-5,

*Then they came to him, bringing a paralytic who was carried by four men. And when they couldn't come near him because of the crowd, they uncovered the roof where he was. So when they had broken through, they let down the*

*bed on which the paralytic was lying. When Jesus saw their faith, he said to the paralytic, "Son, your sins are forgiven you."*

You have just seen four men who used their faith to get their friend healed from being paralyzed. Did you catch what you just read– the four men used their faith? Once again, every man, including you, has a measure of faith! It's totally up to you to develop your measure that was given to you at the new birth. How did the four develop their faith in Jesus? Look at the bottom half of Mark 2:2,

*And he preached the word to them.*

Remember, faith comes by hearing. Hearing what? The word of God. Those four men kept hearing the word that Jesus can heal. They also heard that whenever Jesus healed someone, there was always a part that the person who was going to receive the healing had to do. So what was the four men's part in order to see their friend healed?

That group of friends had love for each other, especially for the one who was paralyzed. We as men must begin to show love towards one another in doing so our faith will increase and we to will experience great over flow of miracles.

When the four heard the word of Jesus they acted on it. How? By going to get their friend who was paralyzed and really believing that Jesus could heal him, and not allowing the circumstances and distractions to stop their faith! For example, they were told the house was too crowded to allow anyone else to come in. They were determined and really believed Jesus was going to heal their friend.

They believed in Jesus and didn't accept no for an answer. They climbed on top of the roof of the house and broke it all up to let down their friend on a bed attached to ropes so that Jesus the ultimate healer could heal their friend.

As a result of the four men doing their part, Jesus then saw something. What was that something? He saw their faith! Not his faith or the woman with the issue of blood's faith! It was their faith that he saw. That's a grand example of the fact that faith can be seen. The four gentlemen's friend was healed from being paralyzed, and was told by Jesus to sin no more. Who were the superheroes in this man's life? It was his four friends, men who operated and used what they had inside them, their faith. There is power in unity and love.

You are a man of faith, that's who you are. Confess who you are on a daily basis. Say to yourself and to others that you are a man of faith! You'll become what you say about yourself. Where you stand right now is a result of what you have spoken or said in your life. So, speak victory!

There's absolutely no reason why you should continue to fail in your life when you have discovered the measure of faith that has been given to you by God. Remember you cannot even please God without your faith. Give your faith a chance to become successful in whatever God has called you to do. You are a superhero, and there are millions of people around you waiting for a superhero to show up on the scene of their troubled lives, but it's going to require the God of your faith to save them from the fears of the world. In doing so, you'll bring great pleasure to God. There is one thing all superheroes have in common, "your faith" 1 John 5:4 says,

*For whatever is born of God overcometh the world. And this is the victory that has overcome the world, your faith.*

Superheroes are world conquerors. They overcome anything that comes their way! That's who you are! You are a world conqueror! You'll always have the victory as long as you do your part, which is to demonstrate your faith!

You can overcome poverty, anger, depression, homosexuality, sexual addictions, and whatever else the world said that you couldn't overcome. You can be a good father to your kids and a good husband to your wife. Divorce isn't God's will! You can overcome a possible divorce situation. You can overcome prison–just do your part. Use your faith.

Your faith, your faith, your faith. Use it! It has been made available for you. Go get the victory, world conqueror.

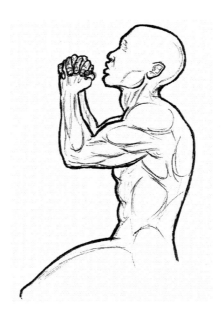

# Chapter Eight

## Super Section One: A place of solitary

*Then he spoke a parable to them, that men always ought to pray and not lose heart. (Luke 18:1)*

Hearing from God and doing what he asks will always bring success. Well! I don't know if the voice I hear is coming from me, the devil, or God. Does that sound like someone you know? God is always speaking, but we are not always listening. One of God's biggest desires is to get the man back into fellowship with him. He wants to answer you back. He wants to help you. He wants and has the best just for you. Anytime there is failure after failure in your life, it's because of two vital reasons:

1. No word of God in your heart
2. No prayer life

For example, say that you had an anger problem and you went into God's word (Bible) to find the answer to your anger problem. If you find the answer, but fail to apply what you know, you will find yourself failing to control your anger. Did you see how the failure occurred in that example? Failure to execute or practice the word of God on any subject of life will produce failure in life. In fact, think about the things that you are failing to do as a man of God. Then you might find out why you are failing. The word of God has to be engraved on your heart before it will work for you.

The other reason for your failures in life would be a lack of a prayer! Prayer is *extremely* important to have in your walk with God. What actually is true prayer? For years and years, traditional teachings told us to just pray about stuff! Everything will be okay. But praying out of fear will short-circuit the prayer's power. True prayer is when you pray from a spirit-filled heart. This is why you spend time getting that word in your heart, so when you pray, you'll be praying back to God the language he understands–his word. And when you pray that word out of faith, you'll see victorious prayers being answered.

Many men struggle with failure in life because they don't know who they are and how effective they could be in their prayer life.

Prayer is your connection line with God. Prayer is a solitary place with God. What is a solitary place, you might ask? It is a place where you can spend time alone with God in prayer. It is a place when you can get answers to the problems that you are facing at the time. This solitary place can be anywhere you choose to feel comfortable to communicate, connect and pray to your father, God. That could be in your car, garage, a personal room, your basement, in a parking lot, on the toilet, it does not matter–just find a place!

Jesus himself prayed often. It was the source of his power. Look with me at Mark 1:35,

> *Now in the morning, having risen a long while before daylight, he went out and departed to a solitary place; and there he prayed.*

In Mark 1, before verse 35, you'll see Jesus being about his father's business: delivering a man from an unclean spirit, healing Simon's mother from a fever, healing and delivering a whole city from various diseases, and casting out many demons. After all this had taken place, everybody was amazed at his power and authority–something that you have, since Jesus lives inside you. But notice one of the major keys to Jesus' successful ministry, in verse 35. It says that Jesus rose early in the morning (maybe in the hours between 3 or 4 o'clock in the morning). He went into a solitary place—a solitary place–and prayed, communicated, and connected with God. Jesus knew how important it was to spend time with God. Every time he did so, he put himself into a position to hear from God and follow through with the instructions that were given to him. Therefore, he was given power from God to carry out the tasks and assignments he received. Right after his prayer session with God, he went right back into fulfilling the perfect will of God for his life. If you'll read Mark 1:39-42, you'll see Jesus displaying his power right after praying, communicating, and connecting with God, as he casts out more demons and heals a man who desired to be cleansed.

Prayer produces power. You are a man who prays, communicates, and connects with God. This is your right! This is who you are. The power that is within you can be stirred up ready to be used in an affective, mighty way when you pray on a consistent basis. Remember, consistency is the key to the breakthrough!

Prayer is a way of life. Without prayer in your life, it is like cutting off your breathing. Likewise, prayer is your spiritual breathing. It will keep your spirit man standing tall inside you. Food is fuel to our bodies to keep us strong and vibrant. Without food we get weak and faint. Without prayer, our spirit man gets faint and is conquered by the flesh. Many men have lost heart in the day of temptation–why? It was because of a lack of prayer. You may say, "Hey, I have temptations every day!" And that can be true, but know that you are not the only man who gets tempted by Satan's evil tactics. Even Jesus Christ himself was tempted. But the question is, "How did Jesus keep from falling into the trap of temptation?" He prayed, he communicated, he connected with God through his spirit man and through praying to the father, his spirit man was more than able to submit to God's instructions and conquer his flesh, which kept him from acting out the temptation. Jesus said in Matthew 26:41,

*Watch and pray, lest you enter into temptation. The spirit indeed is willing, but the flesh is weak.*

You are a man of God who has a spirit, who has a soul (mind), and who lives in a physical body. Your physical body that you see isn't the real you. Your body is just a shell, a covering of your spirit man. Your flesh, which is connected to your mind and your outer body, is the thing that is always warring with your spirit man. Your flesh, which is also your way of thinking instead of God's way of thinking, is always subject to worldly temptations. Your spirit man is always willing to do things God's way. It is at all times willing to move you into the right direction to a fulfilling, prosperous lifestyle. But your spirit man never gets that opportunity—why? Because your flesh needs prayer, communication, and connection to God in order for your spirit man to be willing to help you through life's temptations. Can you see now? Men who struggle with temptations such as drugs, alcohol, smoking, sexual sins, lust, abusive behaviors, and many more are a product of a weak flesh (mind), which is based in a weak prayer life.

If you are struggling with any kind of temptation, you can be sure that a lack of communication, connection, and prayer to God your father is the reason why your spirit is weak. Strengthen your spirit by controlling your flesh! How? By praying. When you do, you'll be winning the war that your spirit man is having against your flesh. If you are tired of being dominated by your flesh, make a quality decision today by taking in the spiritual medication of prayer to defeat temptation. Begin to rise early in the morning and pray, communicate, and connect with God. Establish yourself a solitary place. Jesus said in Luke 22:46,

*Why do you sleep? Rise and pray, lest you enter into temptation.*

Don't allow sleep to rob you of the time that you are to meet with God. Just know that God is waiting for you at your solitary place. He knows that you may be struggling with the temptations of this world. He wants you to communicate and connect with him through your prayers. In return, he'll communicate and connect with you by answering your prayers. Even the answer to temptation is prayer! Notice that the above scripture ordered you to rise and pray lest you enter temptation. Can you now see why the temptations of the world have been ripping the lives of men into shreds? No prayer life! Prayer is a powerful source that you have inside you.

One other problem that could hinder your prayer life is unbelief. For example, you may say, "This temptation causes me to fall every time I'm faced with it. There is absolutely no way that I can stop doing this!" If you can honestly say, "Yes, that's me," then here is a solution to ponder. Do you remember Jesus in the garden of Gethsemane, when it was the hour for him to face death for us? Do you actually think that this hour was easy for Jesus? Not at all, to know that he was about to be killed, no way! He even asked his father to let this cup pass. I'm sure he also thought about telling his father, "I can no longer take this. How about getting my cousin to die for the sins of the world?" Now look at Luke 22:44,

*And being in agony, he prayed more earnestly. Then his sweat became like great drops of blood falling down to the ground.*

The temptation to quit causes Jesus to be in agony. He even prayed earnestly, which means praying from the heart. The temptation was so heavy on him that he sweated great drops of blood that fell to the ground. Now, man of God, allow me to ask you a question. What temptation that you think you cannot conquer has caused you to sweat great drops of blood? Although Jesus did go through all that, he still didn't yield into the temptation of quitting. He passed the test! But where did he get the strength to pass the test? Look again at the first sentence of Luke 22:44,

*He prayed.*

You may say, "Well, that was Jesus!" True; but isn't Jesus living inside of you? Aren't you living in Jesus? Aren't you a joint heir with Christ? Well, if you didn't know–yes! This is who you are in Christ! You have an inheritance of prayer that is waiting to explode like dynamite in every area of your life. Jesus strengthened himself by prayer. No temptation can hold you back if you'll only use what you have! You have the power of prayer, your ability to communicate and connect with God and get the results that you desire for others and yourself. When you begin to tap into the power of prayer, you and people you encounter will know that you know exactly how to get God to move in your life. It won't be long before others will approach you desiring you to pray for them. Why? In their eyes, you are a superhero. In God's eyes you are superhero, and as you continue to read this book, be convinced that you are a man who prays super prayers and gets super evidence from a super God. Make a commitment today! Decide and tell God you are going to meet him faithfully at your chosen solitary place every day. Make a commitment to follow Jesus' example. He simply communicated, connected and prayed to God, and in return received "power" to be a success. Therefore, decide to pray, communicate and connect with God! After all that's who you are, a man of prayer.

## Super Section Two: The power of understanding

*In all your getting, get understanding. (Proverbs 4:7)*

"Just pray about it! Just keep on praying! Everything is going to be all right! Will you please pray for me? You need to pray!" I know that you may have heard these phrases repeatedly. Have you ever just tried to pray about it and then realized you didn't know what to say? Have you ever just tried to keep on praying and stopped after three words, not knowing exactly what to say? Have people approached you, asking you to pray for them, and you were stuck with the words, "Father, I pray that you, um...." Or perhaps your mama or grandmother said to you often, "You need to pray!" But you didn't know how.

Such statements are good, but people often say them religiously, that is, with the usual form but not with any power. Most men don't know how to pray. They pray out of fear instead of faith! Prayers such as "God please, please help me. Lord if you'll just stop by. Dear heavenly Father, I know that I am nothing but a filthy rag; just seeing if you can just bless me," all are what I call wet paper sack prayers! What do you mean, you may ask? If the bottom of a paper sack is wet and you try to load that paper sack up with groceries, everything that was put into that paper sack will fall straight to the ground. Why? Because the bottom of the paper sack is wet–it has no stability, no substance, no solid foundation. The wet paper sack bottom isn't strong enough to hold the groceries. It's the same when you don't understand how to pray effective prayers that will connect to God instead of the ground.

I know that this may sound like your prayer life, but that's going to change based on the information I'm going to give about how to pray.

In the beginning, I mentioned that the only language that God understands when someone prays to him is the language of his word. His language and words are the words that are printed in your Bible. Now, man of God, I am about to give you three steps in showing you how to pray effectively. So, get ready. Before you start reading how to pray

147

effectively, stop and thank God for understanding on how to pray effectively.

Okay, this is who you are. You are a man who understands how to pray effectively.

Open your Bible, the word of God, and whatever you read concerning your or someone else's situation, pray that back to God. For that word or scripture to be highly effective when you pray, put it into your heart. You'll connect with God when you pray from your heart.

Thank God for the answer.

For example, if you need healing in your physical body, go to the word and locate healing scriptures. Here's one,

*By whose stripes you were healed. 1 Peter 2:24*

Another would be,

*Jesus Himself took our infirmities, and bore our sicknesses. Matthew 8:17*

Now begin to meditate on those scriptures every day! Memorize them, confess them to yourself and out loud. The key is making sure those healing scriptures are getting into your heart. It works just like knowing your favorite song by heart—to know that song by heart, you listened to it over and over again, didn't you?

Likewise, take those scriptures and say them over and over again. Then, when you pray, you'll pray with power! Why? You're praying from your heart. When you earnestly pray, that's when you'll see the healing begin. Just simply pray this way from your heart, "Father God, I thank you for healing me. Your word says in 1 Peter 2:24 that by Jesus' stripes I am healed. You also said in your word, according to Matthew 8:17, that Jesus took my infirmities and bore my sicknesses. Therefore, I believe and receive my healing right now in the name of Jesus. Once again thank you for healing me."

When you pray like that from your heart, that's when you are communicating and making contact with God. This is praying effectively, instead of praying out of a heart full of fear, doubt and unbelief. Now keep in mind, this order of prayer goes for any area of life such as finances, debt cancellation, reconciliation, a virtuous, fine wife, deliverance from bondage of a thing, etc. The answer you need is in the word of God. Find that answer and then pray it to God from your heart. That's your right, man of God, to see super results in your prayer life.

Before ending this section of the chapter, I want to go back and expound a little more on a heartfelt prayer, a prayer prayed from your heart. Often, men pray from their mind instead of their heart. So get the word into your heart and then pray that back to God. You may remember at one time in your life where you prayed with all of your heart and God answered that prayer. I surely can remember! I also remember when I prayed out of my mind, and every time I did so I got no results. You are the righteousness of God and once again you have a right for your prayers to produce.

Let's look at two people, a man of God and a woman of God, located in your Bible, and how both got tremendous results from praying from their heart. Look with me at 1Peter 5:17,

*Elijah was a man with a nature like ours. He prayed earnestly that it would not rain; and it didn't rain on the land for three years and six months. And he prayed again, and the heavens gave rain, and the earth produced its fruit.*

Now that's what I call a man with super power. The Prophet Elijah was known to be a superhero. This man had the power to stop the rain and start it! How did he do it, you may ask? He simply prayed earnestly! So when a man is praying earnestly, he prays from the heart. I wonder what will happen in your life, man of God, if you commit to praying earnestly in your everyday prayer life. You may be saying, "Yeah, that's all good, but that was God's prophet." True, that was God's prophet, but God desires to use you in prayer and in the mighty way that he used the Prophet Elijah. God isn't a respecter of persons, but he is a respecter of faith! What he did for one man he'll do for another. As far as prayer is concerned, begin to do what Elijah did to get results in his prayer life–pray earnestly! In other words, pray the word of God from your heart, for in doing so people will see your results, and it won't be long before they begin to see you as a superhero.

Now let's look at another of God's unique creations that always seems to get results when they pray. This unique creation that I'm talking about is called the woman. Whenever a woman prays, she definitely gets results. Well, what's the difference between a man and woman's prayer life, brother Brooks, you may ask? Nothing! It's just the fact that when a woman spends more time with God in prayer, she prays from her heart instead of her mind. Question—when, while you were growing up, did you hear your daddy praying or grandpa praying? It was very seldom for me. I always heard my mama crying out to God, and people say I have a praying grandmother. Women's spirits are more vulnerable to God then men's. This is no excuse at all; we should be more vulnerable towards God as well. Woman will pack out a church and will do all the serving as well. We as men don't like it when women outdo us in a job, career, job skills, etc. But we seem not to have any problems whatsoever when they dominate the leadership positions in the church. That has got to change, men of God. This is the purpose of this book–to show you who you really are in Christ so that you can stand in your rightful position as a man of God. Look with me at 1 Samuel 1:11,

*Then she made a vow and said, "O Lord of hosts, if you'll indeed look on the affliction of your maidservant and remember me, and not forget your maidservant, but will give your maidservant a male child, then I'll give him to the Lord all the days of his life, and no razor shall come upon his head.*

Here is a woman whose womb was barren; she couldn't produce any children at the time. All of the other women were having children except for her. People talked about her and laughed at her because her womb was barren. I can only imagine the pain that she had while others were bearing children, as they laughed and mocked her, "Uh-huh, you cannot have any kids. Where is your God?" Maybe your life is barren right now and others are laughing and mocking you and saying, "Where is your God? You don't have any results in your life. " But now that you are finding out who you are, tell them to keep watching as you apply what you learn from God's word and this book.

So what did Hannah do to get God to move on her behalf? She made a vow to God, as she promised if God gave her a child, that she wouldn't keep him for herself, but would give him back to the Lord. But not only that did she do that! Look at verse 12 and 13,

*And it happened, as she continued praying before the Lord, that Eli watched her mouth. Now Hannah spoke in her heart; only her lips moved, but her voice wasn't heard.*

Hannah not only made a vow, she prayed from her heart, as you see in verse 13. So we see based on the word of God that this woman prayed an earnest prayer to God, not a wet paper sack prayer that was unstable and supported by fear, doubt, and unbelief. By praying from her heart, did she get what she was believing God for? Look with me at verse 20,

*So it came to pass in the process of time that Hannah conceived and bore a son, and called his name Samuel. Saying, "Because I have asked for him from the Lord."*

Wow! God came through again! Why? Because this woman, Hannah, prayed from her heart instead of her mind! Not only that, she kept her part of the vow that she promised God by giving Samuel, her only son, back to God. And look what else God did for her. Look at 1 Samuel 2:21,

*And the Lord visited Hannah, so that she conceived and bore three sons and two daughters. Meanwhile the child Samuel grew before the Lord.*

Not only did the woman everybody laughed at and mocked

have one son, she had five more children–three more sons and two more daughters, a total of six. This is why, man of God, it is so important to know how to pray, communicate and connect with God. In doing so, you'll experience the blessing of God as Hannah did. I myself am communicating to God, making that connection to God on a daily basis with my heart, and changes are being made and blessing is being manifested in my life.

You now know how to pray effectively. Begin to practice praying from your heart instead of your mind. This will yield you great results in your prayer life, and other men will no longer be laughing but will be looking at you in awe as they see you standing tall and prosperous–the superhero that you are. Can you see now how understanding makes a big difference?

## Super Section Three: Spiritual weapons for spiritual wars

*How shall we escape if we neglect so great a salvation? (Hebrews 2:3)*

As men of God, we must take inventory of ourselves on a consistent basis. To evaluate your walk in Christ will always open that door to reality in certain areas of your life.

You are reading about one particular area, which concerns your relationship with God. That's prayer life. Many men never escape failure's grasp because they neglect that part of their spiritual life. When you pray the way that you learned in Section Two, you'll also be confessing the word of God back to God. In fact, if there's no prayer, there's no confession. If there's no confession, there's no prayer. Then how can you escape the darts Satan throws at you? Deadly darts of sickness and disease, of car wrecks and plane crashes, of fear, of failure and poverty— all the deadly darts that are under the law of sin and death.

For example, if you never spend time confessing and praying for God's protection over your life, chances are you'll leave a window open for Satan. In addition, when bad things happen, we ask God why? And He'll always be glad to answer through His word by saying, "You neglect so great a salvation, how can you escape?"

Please understand, men of God, it wasn't God who got you evicted. God is a good God and he's a God of love (you'll read more about the love of God in Chapter 9). God came to give you an abundant life, not an abandoned life! A life abounding with joy and peace.

While in prison, I met a quiet man. He'd always walk past me and look at me as if he were begging, "I need someone to talk too!" One day, when things were slow at the laundry, I went outside and stood on the loading dock. As I stood there, he approached me and we started talking. As the conversation continued, he began pouring out his heart to me. Like many men, he had many unanswered questions. Just by looking at him and hearing him talk you could tell his understanding was clouded. He was a big, white man, very intelligent. Therefore, I asked him, "What's the biggest question you'd ask God, if he were talking to you?"

He said, "I'd ask God why he took my mother away from me." He went on, "She was a good person. She didn't curse, smoke, do drugs or do anything wrong! She always did good things. As soon as she got sick, He let her die! Why?"

I said, "That's a good question. Many people ask why God did this or that.

I then asked, "How did your mom die?"

He said, "She died of a heart attack."

"Do you know what led to the heart attack?" I asked.

He replied, "Yes, x-rays showed that her arteries were clogged up with grease. The doctor told her to stop eating so much greasy food, because if she continued she could develop heart disease. My mom tried to mellow out, but she just couldn't stop. A year and a half later she had the heart attack!"

I then asked him to listen to me carefully. And his attention was there. So I asked God for the wisdom to give him the answer he needed.

I said, "Man, God didn't kill your mother. A heart attack killed your mother. The enemy, which is Satan, comes to kill, steal and destroy. God comes to give you life and abundance through his son, Jesus Christ. Your mother ignored the doctor's orders. Therefore, she developed heart disease and that was what killed her, not God. God used the doctor to warn her. I can imagine when she learned about her bad heart worry, doubt and fear was there."

He said, "Yes, sir. She was that way."

I then said, "If faith was there to believe that God loves her so much that he could heal her, she'd have given him permission to help her out by healing her body. Fear only pleases Satan. But you can get God to do anything if you'll please him–how? By using your faith! Then God can do what the doctors said was impossible and make it possible. It wasn't God; it was heart disease that caused your mother's death."

Tears streamed down his face. "Thank you, I understand."

As days went on, I made sure he understood God doesn't kill, steal or destroy. Satan does that. Please, men of God, don't allow procrastination, slothfulness, laziness or fear to keep you from confessing and praying God's word over your life and your friends' and family's lives.

If so, you could end up saying, "How can I escape if I neglect so great a salvation?"

There's a spiritual battle that's probably going on in your daily walk with Christ. Satan himself is initiating it. Why does Satan go so hard after the man of God?

He knows if you ever realize who you are in Christ, you'll be a dangerous threat to his kingdom—the kingdom of darkness.

He knows that if your heart is filled with God's word, prayer manifestation is inevitable.

Satan is always sending out spiritual wars against spirit-filled believers. He also knows the spiritual power behind prayers from the heart. He doesn't want to see that power yield any results. He sends spiritual and physical attacks, to make you believe your prayers won't work. Nevertheless, praise God, because he's given us weapons—spiritual weapons that defeat his wars! There are four spiritual weapons of prayer, which are powers that are inside you ready and willing to be used at the time of battle:

1. The prayer of agreement
2. The prayer of binding and loosing
3. The prayer of faith
4. The prayer of intercession

Now, let's look at each of these weapons of prayer. Locate how each of these weapons of prayer can be effective during a spiritual war. Remember, you're learning who you are—a man of effective prayer!

## "The Prayer of Agreement"

Whenever there's a spiritual war, it would be wise to find another brother or brothers in the Lord. Come together and agree on whatever you are asking God for. Ask with confidence. This type of prayer will always bring victory. Let's look into the word of God and see God's benefits when you pray in agreement. Look at Matthew 18:19-20,

*Again, I say to you that if two of you agree on earth concerning anything that they ask, it will be done. For where two or three are gathered together in my name. I am there in the midst of them.*

There are others in agreement with you. When you come together and pray in the name of Jesus, you give him permission to stand in agreement with you as well. Therefore, how can you ever lose again, when Jesus Christ, the anointed one, is standing with you? Where there's no agreement, there's no unity. Where there's no unity, there's confusion, and when there's confusion, you'll find failure. But there's power in agreement.

## "The Prayer of Binding and Loosing"

Another weapon available to you during spiritual warfare is the prayer of binding and loosing. This type of prayer is one of the keys that Jesus himself died for. He went into the pits of hell and snatched them out of the hands of Satan. Jesus has given you the key to unlock the power of binding and loosing anything that has had you, your family or friends bound up or held tightly by the schemes of Satan. Jesus said in Matthew 16:19,

*And I'll give you the keys of the kingdom of heaven, and whatever you bind on earth will be bound in heaven, and whatever you loose on earth will be loosed in heaven.*

Question—Why would Jesus give us (men of God) the keys of binding and loosing negative things that are in our life or in the lives of others? Jesus understands the reality of spiritual warfare. You have the ability to bind up any evil spirit that tries to war with you. When you take authority and bind up an evil spirit that is working against you, you are giving all of heaven the authority to bind up that evil spirit based on the prayer you prayed to bind up a thing.

Anyone that is allowing the enemy to use them in an evil way towards you can also be bound up through the prayer of binding and loosing. So if someone on the job, in a grocery store, in traffic, in your family, at your local church or wherever you spend time around people, is being used by the enemy, just know it's not the person—it's the spirit behind the person. So don't ever retaliate against them, retaliate against the spirit that's causing them to war against you. How? By praying the prayer of binding and loosing! Just simply pray, "Father, your word says that I have the key of binding and loosing according to Matthew 16:19. Therefore, in the name of Jesus I bind up that spirit that's working through such and such, that is warring against me, and I command all maneuvers (actions) to cease right now, in the name of Jesus."

Once you have prayed this type of prayer, praying the word, all of heaven will be there to back you up, and whatever you bind on earth will be bound in heaven. Just keep in mind, you have the power to bind up anything that tries to come up against you. The evil spirit will stop warring against you, if you'll only use what you've got.

You also have the weapon of prayer for loosing any negative situation in you or around you just as much as any positive situation that will concern you. For example, you may need a financial miracle. The bills are due, they are talking about foreclosing on your house, and they're repossessing your truck and your motorcycle. What do you do? You say to yourself, "I can't get a loan–my credit is bad and my debt is all I have to show for my progress." It's now time to use your key that Jesus gave you. You have the power to loose a financial miracle from heaven. How? By praying the word back to God concerning your finances, "Father, you said in Philippians 4:19 that you'll supply all of my needs according to your riches and glory, and I take authority right now by loosing finances in the name of Jesus. I loose it here on earth, therefore it is loosed in heaven."

Please understand–when God looses money he won't get off his throne, have you stick your hand out, and drop $5. Instead, he'll work on the hearts of people. Also keep this fact near and dear to your heart–you cannot beat God giving so always have a generous heart of giving yourself. Sow seeds of finance and you'll always reap a harvest of finances. Cover yourself by doing this, so when the wind of lack and need blows your way, you'll be established to use the power of loosing because of the financial seed that you have sown.

Money isn't the only thing that you can loose from heaven. You can loose healing and deliverance in your physical body or someone else's. Look with me at Luke 13:11-13,

*And behold, there was a woman who had a spirit of infirmity eighteen years, and was bent over and could in no way raise herself up. But when Jesus saw her, he called her to him and said to her, Woman, you are loosed from your infirmity.*

You see, here's Jesus speaking healing over this woman's physical body by saying, "Woman, you are loosed from your infirmity." You, man of God, have the super power to loose anything that's negative in or outside your physical body, whether that is you or someone else. You may say, "Well, brother Brooks, that was Jesus! There is no way I could do such a thing." Well, if Jesus is living inside you, you can do what he does. Here's proof. Look at Romans 8:17,

*And if children, then heirs-heirs of God and joint heirs with Christ.*

If you are a Christian, Jesus is in you. He is always 24/7 living inside you. You can do what he did and have what he has–why? You and Jesus are one. Once you get the reality that Jesus really does live inside you, and that you can do what he does, you'll no longer live an average lifestyle but a super lifestyle. So if Jesus can loose anything, you can too, because you understand that you are a joint heir with Christ. Besides, Jesus was the one who gave you the keys to binding and loosing!

So now, your prayer life has been enhanced because of the weapons of prayer of binding and loosing. If you pray this way, it won't be long before you start seeing the super results of the supernatural God that you serve. You only become what you serve, so continue to serve God so that you can live permanently in the supernatural by applying all the weapons of prayer.

### "The Prayer of Intercession"

This weapon of prayer is the reason you and I are still alive today! If it hadn't been for grandmama or mama or some other loved one applying the weapon of the prayer of intercession, where exactly *would* we be today? The prayer of intercession is a type of prayer that gets involved in the life of another person or people. It is designed to intercept any demonic spiritual attack that is maneuvering to steal, kill and destroy.

Men of God, this type of prayer is so important to learn about because it deals with the lives of others. When a man begins praying for others concerning their needs, wants and desires, that's when God will begin to take care of *your* needs, wants and desires. Here is a prime example of the power of intercessory prayer.

As you already know, Job lost everything that he owned, not because God took everything from him or even allowed Satan to take everything from him. It was Job's fear that caused him to lose everything he had or owned, as it shows in Job 3:26. Men of God, once again, this is a lesson for us all not to fear! In doing so, you could lose everything you own.

Now, I want us to focus on the last chapter of Job, chapter 42. We know that Job lost everything, but if you'll read the whole chapter of Job 42, you'll see that everything was restored to him twice as much as than he had the first time. The question is, "How did he get more than he lost?" Look with me at Job 42:10. Here is the secret to Job's restoration:

*And the Lord restored Job's losses when he prayed for his friends. Indeed the Lord gave Job twice as much as he had before.*

Did you catch the secret to Job's restoration? It was Job praying for his friends. That's how he gained twice what he had lost. In other words, Job interceded on behalf of his friends. Can you see the power behind interceding, praying for someone other than yourself? You may have loved ones that are not serving the Lord. They may be in the same place where you were when you were lost. Even though you were addicted to drugs, alcohol, pornography, a drug dealer, a woman beater, suicidal, in a gang, a robber and thief in the corporate world, or in the streets in any other kind of mess that you were in, you found God eventually in it all. How? Someone was praying for you. You see, men of God, in order to get him involved in the affairs of others such as relatives or friends; you have give him something to work with. And that would have to be your prayers interceding for their salvation and protection.

Every time there's a sudden death, God wonders at that, because if there had been an intercessor, that prayer alone would have given God a chance to work out the situation. Look with me at Isaiah 56:16,

*He saw that there was no man, and wondered that there was no intercessor.*

This is a powerful weapon made available for you. You can always fight the devil off your loved ones, friends and even people you don't know, when you pray and intercede for them. The reason why you are not yet dead and are reading this book to get empowered as you find out who you are in Christ, is the same reason that you loved ones, friends, etc. won't die without Christ–because of the weapon of prayer called intercession.

Gentlemen, begin right now to practice this! You have the ability to get God to get involved with someone else's needs, wants, desires, safety and protection through your prayers of intercession. Remember, when you pray with others' best interests at heart, God will turn around and see about your best interests. You saw him do it for Job. He can do it for you, if you'll only do what Job did, to simply pray or intercede for others. Job looked like a superhero in the eyes of his friends and his acquaintances after Job's storm. Man of God, your day is coming! Continue to find out who you are and apply it!

## "The Prayer of Faith"

Here is one of the most powerful prayers a man can pray. The reason I say that it's the most important is because for any of the other prayers to be effective, you must have faith. Not to downplay those three forms of prayer, which you are going to need in your everyday life. But the weapon of prayer that you can be sure to win with in any spiritual war is the prayer of faith. Look with me at 1 Peter 5:15,

*And the prayer of faith will save the sick, and the Lord will raise him up. And if he has committed sins, he'll be forgiven.*

Notice what the prayer of faith will do–save the sick and raise them up. But that's not all the prayer of faith can do. The prayer of faith can create a promotion; it can restore your marriage or your relationships; it can prosper you in whatever you do and cause you to live like a king as you were born to do. The prayer of faith can cause deliverance from prison and the issues of life. And I'm talking about the negative issues of life that keep a man in bondage.

This whole chapter was designed to show you the power of prayer that is invested inside you. You also read in chapter seven about faith, and now we're reading about the prayer of faith. The prayer of faith is designed to get ultimate results in your life. We understand that prayer is communicating and connecting and fellowshipping with God by acting on the word of God. When you pray the word of God and act on it you develop confidence in that prayer, knowing that God will answer your prayer because it was birthed out of a heart full of faith. This is why it's so very important, man of God, to get the word in your heart, so that you can pray what's in your heart. Faith is supposed to always abide–live--in your heart, without doubt or fear. What happens when you pray and you don't get the desired results? Look with me at James 1:6-8,

*But let him ask in faith, with no doubting, for he who doubts is like a wave of the sea driven and tossed by the wind. For let not that man suppose that he'll receive anything from the Lord; he is a double -minded man, unstable in all his ways.*

When you ask God for something, it's the same as praying for something. Many Christian men are not receiving the answers to their prayer, not because they did something wrong or God is mad at them. It could simply be because of a lack of faith in that prayer or whatever you are asking God for. The Bible says that man shouldn't suppose that he'll receive anything from the Lord. Why? Why can't a man receive anything form the Lord, including an answered prayer? Because of a heart full of doubt and unbelief along with a double mind–a mind that thinks one minute, I know that I can win and within the next ten minutes thinks, I'm not sure if I can win! So you continue to live a life of wavering and find yourself tossed by the winds of disappointment, depression, and low self-esteem, it's all because of the wind of failure created by fear.

Often Christians pray the prayer of faith, but still don't receive, why? Look with me at James 4:3,

*You ask and do not receive, because you ask wrongly, in order to spend what you get on your pleasures.*

So what is the cause of asking or praying amiss? It is praying the wrong motive. I've prayed prayers that weren't answered. It was disappointing to feel rejected by God. It wasn't the fact that God was rejecting me; it was because I had the wrong motive. For example, I remember praying and asking God to give this certain lady to me to be my wife. God never did it. Why? Because God doesn't give you a mate; he can approve of your choice but never choose for you. Why? Because you are a free moral agent and she is as well and God gave you both the power of choice. To be honest with you, I really just wanted to have sex with her; I was simply lusting after her. That was my motive and therefore, I prayed amiss.

Evaluate your prayers before you pray them. The prayer of faith does work, but only when you pray along with the word of God. Always check the motive behind whatever you wish to do. I have heard of ministers who went into the ministry just for the sake of the money instead of the people, and their ministries fell to the ground. Why? Their motive was wrong.

Praise God, you are no longer a man who will ask amiss when you pray, because you understand how to evaluate your motives, and not to doubt or be tossed by the winds of the negative issues of life. You will stand firm on the foundation of the prayer of faith.

# Chapter Nine

## Super Section One: The heroic force that never fails

*The love of God has been poured into our hearts through the Holy Spirit that has been given to us. (Romans 5:5)*

Superheroes are all motivated by saving someone or something. They're extremely courageous. They have absolutely no doubt or an ounce of fear about their capabilities. As you were growing up watching cartoons of Superman, Batman, Spiderman, He-Man, and reading comic books on Captain America and the X-Men, you saw that these superheroes took great pride in what they did. Now, I know just as well as you that these heroic characters are all fiction, but if you pay attention, you can learn a lot as far as morals and values are concerned.

For example, what motivated Superman to save the little boy from trouble? Why did Spiderman save the little old lady from a wild-headed robber? What motivated Batman to save a whole city from being destroyed? There had to be some kind of force that motivated them to commit themselves to dangerous situations that could cost them their very lives. Just for a moment, I'd like to step back into the world of reality and ask you the same question. What actually motivates today's heroes such as a firefighter, a police officer, or a security officer? What is the force behind United States Marines or Navy Seals who put their lives on the line just for us in a devastating war where bullets fly inches away from striking them in the head, heart, or leg?

And what about you? I know that, some time in your life, you have committed some kind of heroic act. You may even commit them every day towards family and friends. Notice I said family and friends, especially the family. Here's a question that I'd like for you to evaluate and answer for yourself. Does your son(s) or daughter(s) look up to you as a superhero father? Does your wife ever congratulate you for being the superhero in her life? If you are demonstrating the life of a superhero in your household, what's motivating you? What is the force that's pushing you to do these heroic acts? That should have been a hint for the answer to the question that I have been asking from the start of this chapter.

My spiritual father, Creflo Dollar, is definitely a superhero in my eyes as well as many other people's. For both of us, "people" are our purpose for living. We both have been gifted by God to impact the lives of people with the word of God and giving understanding in how to apply the word to people's everyday lives. Dr. Creflo Dollar has two mega churches: one in Atlanta, GA of 26,000 members, and another in New York City of 6,000 members, both rapidly growing. He also travels throughout the United States and other nations proclaiming the gospel, which is the good news. He can be seen on television as much as "I Love Lucy" and the "Andy Griffith Show

And as you already know, this book is designed to wake up the inner man. How? By discovering that the inner man really is Christ Jesus. The lives of people are what we're after. You and other men are the heartbeat of God! Jesus Christ, "the anointed one," died for you and me so that we both could be a part of God's heartbeat. Now that's a heroic act!!!

Cartoon superheroes, superheroes of the police force, fire department, the U.S. Armed Forces, teachers, lawyers, preachers, authors, and a host of others (especially fathers), God himself and Jesus are the superheroes who are motivated, who operate under a force that causes a superhero to never fail. That motivational force is called "love."

The day that you invited Jesus Christ and the presence of the Holy Spirit to sit down on the throne of your heart was the day that the seed of love was poured into your heart. You are a man of love! The seed of love is hovering in your heart, waiting to be released on someone. You may have said, "Oh, no! I'm not a man of love. I can honestly say I'm unforgiving. I'm angry. I still hate such and such for cheating on me. I have a bad temper. My attitude is very impatient. No, not me–I can't love anyone." Such statements are not true about you but such actions may be true in your life. That's because your cure has not yet been exercised or cultivated. That's the seed of love.

When you came forth out of your mother's womb, your arms had tiny bicep muscles. As you grew, they grew, and when you got older, you may have desired to develop those bicep muscles into bigger and stronger muscles. So, in order to do so, you had to go into a weight room and apply extreme pressure to your biceps by using weights and machines to cause your biceps to grow into your desired result. It's the same when you want to stop being angry, unforgiving, flying off the handle over everything, impatient, mean to others such as your wife or children. Begin to exercise that muscle of love that's already inside you.

You may ask, "How do I exercise my muscle of love?" Simple–just do what love does! So what does love do? Look with me at 1 Corinthians 13:4-8,

*Love suffers long and is kind; love does not envy; love does not parade itself, isn't puffed up; does not behave rudely, does not seek its own, isn't provoked, thinks*

*no evil; does not rejoice in iniquity, but rejoices in the truth; bears all things, believes all things, hopes all things, endures all things. Love never fails.*

In this scripture, you can see the dos and the don'ts of love. Let's look at the dos of love and apply them to your everyday life. If you consistently do so, you'll never have to worry about the don'ts!

o **Love is patient.** Start being patient with others. Keep in mind that God was and is still patient with you. Look for opportunities to be patient; in doing so you are practicing, exercising your love muscle.

o **Love is kind.** Instead of being mean and hateful, just begin to be kind. Keep telling yourself, "I'm a kind man. I won't be mean. I'll practice being a kind man."

o **Love bears all things.** Just as an umbrella bears the rain and protects you from getting wet, love bears up under all things. You can bear up under any evil situation that comes your way! Anything that is evil, just say, "No! I am not going to let that get to me. I'll get through this!" Begin to practice bearing up under all things. Nothing can stop or hurt you when you operate in the love of bearing up under all things.

o **Love believes all things.** Love believes the best! Even about your enemies. Love also believes in you, so if love is in you, you believe in you. Begin to believe in God's word. Take him at his word! If he said that he'd give you the desires of your heart, believe it! Believe that you, your family and others will prosper. Begin to practice believing all good things.

o **Love hopes all things.** "Hope deferred makes the heart sick, but a desire fulfilled is a tree of life." (Proverbs 13:12) Through hoping in God's word, your desires can come to pass in your life. Likewise, hope for all good things to happen in another's life, that's love.

o **Love endures all things.** Love never gives up! If you feel like that you are at the end of the rope and you want to let go, don't do it! Don't give up! Why? Because love endures even in the worst of times. You and the marriage will win because love endures. Don't let go of your dreams, your own business, or whatever it may be–hold on! That's what love does–it endures. There may be people in your life that are hard to deal with and that's good. Why? They are your exercising equipment to make love endure. Use them to practice your love walk.

The look-at-me attitude, the rude behavior, the self-seeking attitude, the provoking attitude, the negative and evil thinking, the rejoicing over the fall of others—those are all the don'ts of love. Men with these attitudes, and men who are subject to anger, malice, strife, etc., are motivated by a force other than love, and that is the force of selfishness. In fact, these are the two most powerful forces on the planet earth: love and selfishness. You are either operating in love or operating in selfishness.

Selfishness is the reason why men want out of marriages–so they can go out and gratify the flesh! Men get very angry when they don't get their way (like I used to) because of selfishness. Think about that. Both love and selfishness have the ability to yield great results. If you have been bringing in negativity in and around your life, check out what force that has been moving you into a negative lifestyle.

All of the negativity can stop right now in your life. You have discovered that you have a seed of love inside your heart. Take advantage of what's inside you. Love is there, love is there, and love is there.

What's moving you? Evaluate yourself! Look at your life and you'll be able to see if the force of love has been moving you or the force of selfishness has been moving you. What moved Jesus? He's our example, right! He's our hero! Wouldn't you agree? Look with me at Mark 1:40-42,

> Now a leper came to him, imploring him, kneeling down to him and saying to him, "If you are willing, you can make me clean." Then Jesus, moved with compassion, stretched out his hand and touched him, and said to him, "I am willing; be cleansed." As soon as he had spoken, immediately the leprosy left him, and he was cleansed.

Here's a leper who desired to be cleansed. Not only that, he knew that in order to be cleansed, he had to contact a superhero that he heard about in the city he lived in. The Bible says that he came to Jesus kneeling down, asking the superhero if he could heal him. As you have read, the superhero healed that man of his deadly condition. However, the question to you was, "What was the force that Jesus, the ultimate superhero, used to bring healing in this man's life?" It was compassion, which is another name for "love." It was the force of love that moved Jesus to heal this man.

All through the Bible, you can find biblical characters, which appeared to be superheroes in the eyes of others. One character was Moses, who led the children of Israel out of bondage into the Promised Land. Although he had trying times, he was moved by "love."

David defeated the giant, Goliath, by putting him on his back! Why? Because of his "love" for God's covenant people and their freedom. When you are committed to operating in "love," you'll always have great rewards.

Joseph was sold into slavery by his own blood brothers, went from the darkness of prison to the splendor of the royal palace, but still was moved by the power of "love" to forgive his brothers, who hated him. He was able to be a blessing in all their lives during a major famine. Now that's what you call love that endures.

You are no different from Moses, David and Joseph. You have the same force inside you that led these men to success, but watch this, Moses had a temper problem, David had a lust issue, and Joseph had an impatience matter. All three had a weakness of the flesh, yet they overcame them. How? By exercising the seed of the muscle called love. All made a change and all became successful because they made their minds up to be forced, moved, and controlled by the power of love.

My objective in this first section of Chapter Nine was for you to discover that the seed of love was poured into your heart the day that you chose the father, the son, and the Holy Ghost to move into your life. God is love and love is God. God will never fail because the Bible says in 1 Corinthians 13:8,

*Love never fails.*

So if God is love and love never fails, and the seed of love is inside you—that would make you a man who can't fail in any arena of your life, because in whatever you do you'll be motivated, forced, by the super power of love.

Now we know the secret of success behind the cartoon superheroes and real superheroes that exist in today's world. As you begin to practice developing your love, you'll see the awesome results behind the force of love. I did it in prison and the results were tremendous. Trust me—people will come to you and ask, "Why are you succeeding with so much favor? How do you do it?" You'll begin to look like the superhero that you are in their eyes, the world's eyes. And you'll be able to answer, "I am a man that is motivated—forced–by the power of love that has been poured into my heart."

# Super Section Two: You have had it your way–now do it God's way

*Yet, I show you a more excellent way. (1 Corinthians 12:31)*

Failure, depression, confusion, and frustration are only a few symptoms of a man who is extremely determined to do things his way. The Bible calls this type of man the prideful man. As you already know, the prideful man always falls into the pit of selfishness, not willing to grab hold of the rope of change and pull his way up out the selfish pit.

When you do things your way instead of God's way, you'll find yourself falling out of an airplane without a parachute to let you glide safely to the ground. You will fall like Satan from the heavens to the stony pit of a hard lifestyle. If you are living or have been living a life full of torment and unnecessary agony, it's because you've been doing things your way! Man of God, you don't have to continue to live that way. I was saved, filled with the Holy Ghost, going to church every time the church doors opened, but still was living a very, very, miserable life. Why? I was so focused and dependent on doing things my way, instead of doing things God's way. You may ask, "What *is* God's way?"

God's way is the most excellent way–the "love way." God is a God of excellence. Who he is, the way he does things—it's all rooted and grounded in love. Without living in the most excellent way, you are really nothing! Now, please don't get upset with me about the statement you just read. I didn't say that–the word did! I'm just a messenger. By the inspiration of the Holy Ghost, I wrote this book to reveal to you the most excellent way. Look with me at 1Corinthians 13:1-3,

*Though I speak with the tongues of men and of angels, but have not love, I have become sounding brass or a clanging cymbal. And though I have the gift of prophecy, and understand all mysteries and all knowledge, and though I have all faith, so that I could remove mountains, but have not love, I am nothing. And though I bestow all my goods to feed the poor, and though I give my body to be burned, but have not love, it profits me nothing.*

As you can see, I didn't say you were nothing. The Apostle Paul through the scriptures said so. He said even if you prayed in other tongues or had great faith to remove mountains or gave everything you had to feed the poor, without living in God's excellent way, which is "love," you are nothing.

Through this book, you have discovered the super powers that

166

your heavenly father, God, has invested inside you. You have realized that imagination and words can work for you. You are the righteousness of God. You have a covenant with God. You have all authority and dominion on the earth, a very powerful force of faith, and the power of prayer to get results. But none of these super powers will work for you unless you are rooted and grounded in God's way, the more excellent way, "love."

Love is the vine, while the power to dominate, prayer, your righteousness, and the rest of God's super powers are the branches. Without the vine the branches will die. So likewise, without love, the powers that are in you are dead and ineffective in your life. In Chapter Seven, you read and understood that you have the power of faith ready to go to work for you. However, what will short-circuit that faith? Look with me in Galatians 5:6 which reads,

*... faith working through love.*

As you can see, your faith can't work for you without your love life working through you.

Just like many of you, I didn't love myself, therefore, it was impossible for me to love others. No wonder my faith didn't work for me! Why? I wasn't allowing my faith to work through love, God's most excellent way. I was always doing it my way, and my way always leads me to turmoil, grief and failure. My way cost me a year and three months in the State Penitentiary! Although my intentions were good, there still was a law that I had to abide under and the Bible, God's way, does say that I must obey the law of the land. I should have done that until (watch this) God's most excellent way was perfected. Take it from me–doing it your way can get you in some serious trouble.

So why do men just want to do it their way? The reason is ever since childhood, the majority of men have been trained to do it their way, which is actually the world's way. The prisons are loaded with men who wanted to do it their way. The graveyard is full of so much talent, potential, and men who died before their time because they were so determined to handle matters their way. The body of Christ itself is congested with men who decided to go through with a divorce, leaving children behind and the weaker vessel to do *his* God-ordained job. Why? Just so he could please himself, which is selfish. How? It's selfish because he's doing it his way.

Let's look at some of man's ways. Since birth, you have been trained by the world to:

• Hate and harm your enemies (Matthew 5:43)

- Pay back or take revenge on someone who has done evil to you (Romans 12:17)

- Practice adultery, fornication, uncleanness, lewdness, idolatry, sorcery, hatred, contention, jealousy, outbursts of wrath, selfish ambitions, dissensions, heresies, envy, murders, drunkenness, wild parties (Galatians 5:20).

But after the new birth, you are to be trained by God's word to:

- Love your enemies and do good to those who persecute you (Matthew 5:44)
- Overcome evil with good (Romans 12:21)

- Practice the fruit of the Spirit, which is your character: love, joy, peace, longsuffering, kindness, goodness, faithfulness, gentleness, and self-control (Galatians 5:22)

Notice the ways of man and the ways of God are all located in the word of God. I know that there are many of you who desire to discontinue doing things your way and really live a life of doing things God's way. Well, the good news is that you can! You can change from doing things your old ways and develop into doing things God's way, which is the most excellent way. Yes, you can find all of God's ways in the Bible. God is love and love is the foundation to all of God's ways.

Accountability towards one another is another one of God's ways. Why as brothers do we fight, snitch, and backbite? brothers remember that there is no sense in being jealous towards one another. If someone lives in a bigger house than you right now, that's okay. There's a bigger and better house somewhere out there just for you. If someone has a beautiful girlfriend or wife hanging on his arm, be happy for him and know that there's a beautiful girl or potential wife out there for you. If someone has a higher-paying job than you do right now, rejoice! Because you know it won't be long before you target *your* dream career or job. If you see someone flourishing in their calling that God has called them to, don't start hating and get all frustrated by trying to find something wrong with their ministry. You just focus on what God has called *you* to do, and you'll see the hand of God in your divine calling from God. Look with me in Ephesians 5:1,

*Therefore be imitators of God as dear children. And walk in love, as Christ also has loved us and given himself for us, an offering and a Sacrifice to God for a sweet-smelling aroma.*

Now that's what has gotten us in so much trouble, and I'm not just talking about the law. I'm speaking of both spiritual and natural life. We've been imitating the wrong characters. We grew up wanting to be like the biggest dope dealer who ever lived, or the biggest athletic star, movie star, rap star that ever existed. Men have carried that same mentality over into their new, born-again experience and desired to imitate pastor such and such or evangelist John Doe instead of being and imitator of God. Now let me explain–it isn't wrong to have characteristics of a pastor you follow or an evangelist that you serve. Just keep it all in perspective. You follow the God in them and develop in imitating the ways of God instead of imitating someone else without God. You are your own man and God expects it to be that way. If someone does wrong you, imitate the way that God would respond! Forgive them and give to them. You are a man of God and a man of God does not have to defend himself. If you'll imitate God by showing and giving love, you'll never have to defend yourself. Why? The love of God that you are imitating will defend itself for you.

Remember, man of God, love never fails! Love people like God loves people. I remember how God spoke to my heart while in prison and said, "Keith, I'd like for you to start practicing loving people unconditionally, just like I do you." I was hungry for the power of faith to work in my life. I was thirsty for the blessing of God to be made manifest in all that I do. The price was walking in unconditional love for people. It was hard because the people in prison are hard to love. But I got better and better, and I began to see changes in my life as well as the effective power of love being demonstrated in the lives of others. When you change, other people change. I am now experiencing the favor of God upon my life like never before, and it's all because I made a decision to no longer do things my way but God's way, the most excellent way, which is the way of love.

Love is the power that is inside you. Once it's been cultivated, rooted and grounded into the depths of your heart, all of the powers of God inside of you will come alive and rise up in you. When you handle things God's way instead of your way, you put yourself in a position to receive more than you can imagine to receive from God, more than you can ask from God, more than you can dream from God. Look at Ephesians 3:20,

*Now to him who is able to do exceedingly abundantly above all that we ask or think, according to the power that works in us.*

I'm telling you, God truly wants to do exceedingly abundantly more than every desire in your heart. But notice, this blessing from God only comes according to the power that desires to work in you. Do you know what that power is? You are correct! That power is the power of love–God's most excellent way.

# Super Section Three: The hero and his father

*My father and I are one. (John 10:30)*

It is very well known that the bloodline of the father is also in the bloodline of the child. As you can see in the above scripture, Jesus announces that he and his father (God) are one, meaning that they are knitted and fitted together in the realm of the Spirit. The very instant that you gave your life to Jesus Christ, the blood of Jesus was injected into your bloodline, overpowering the bloodline of your natural father. I must agree that many men suffer from the effects of having the bloodline of their fathers, but that's only if their bloodline was full of evil instead of the goodness of purity.

Therefore, what happens if my father was a very corrupt person? What if I did all the wrong things he did and more? I mean, after all, his blood and mine are one! This may be a fact. Maybe he abused women, or he has a child in each of the 50 states, or he was a thief. He did this! He did that! Whether negative or positive, there is a cycle of doing things the way that your father did. However, the blood of Jesus cleanses your old natural bloodline and produces a new one. It's a bloodline that I call type "G". In other words, you're a god or a product of God. Notice the small "g." I didn't say you are God, but an offspring of God making you a little "g." That's who you are. You're a god on the planet.

Allow me to prove it! Remember that you don't have to believe a word that I've written. However, please believe the Holy Bible, the word of God. Look with me at John 10:34,

*Is it not written in your law? "I said, 'you are gods'?"*

Keep in mind, the one who just made this statement by asking a question was Jesus, himself. (He begins talking in verse 32.) Now look with me in Psalms 82:6,

*I said. "You are gods, and all of you are children of the most high."*

So from reading that verse, what makes you a god? How do you become a god in this earth? What right do you have to call yourself a god? You simply exchange bloodlines from your natural father over to your spiritual father by giving your life to Jesus Christ, the injection button that causes you and your ultimate father to become one.

This is the answer to destroying the cursed ways of your natural father, eliminating that old pattern of thinking that you were raised with of being "just like your daddy." If your biological father was a loser and did evil things that caused hurt and shame to you or others, it does not mean that you have to be that way. You are now a Son of God. You are a child of the most High! You do things totally differently than your father. Think about you being a "god." You are a very, very, powerful man–full of the power of God. God didn't place you here on earth to make the same mistakes your father made; you were put here for a holy purpose!

"Yeah, but you don't understand–my mother was raped and after I was born I was abandoned." I'm sorry to hear that, but God isn't sorry because he knew you when you were in your mother's womb! You are not a mistake–God doesn't make mistakes. He specializes in building up men who were convinced that they were a mistake or made too many mistakes. God builds them up, shows them who they really are, and turns them into superheroes. In 1 Corinthians 1:28,

*And the base things of the world and the things which are despised God has chosen, and the things which are not, to bring to nothing the things that are.*

Okay, you have been despised, hurt, wounded, misunderstood, talked about, etc. That should be good news! According to the scripture you just read, somebody had to be despised first before God could choose them. For if no one was ever despised, what would God have to choose from? God has chosen you, man of God. Now since he has chosen you, begin to choose him and his ways as your father, so that you can put to shame the wise as you stand proudly in the shadow of your heavenly father as a superhero.

I remember a time in my life where I felt so awful, so confused because I didn't have a loving father. I didn't have someone who could show me how to catch a football, how to treat a woman, or how to do my homework. There were times when the other guys' dads would be at the track meet supporting their sons with cheers and tips on how to get better, when all I could do was look around and think how nice it would be to have a caring father.

This is why it is so important, gentlemen, to be a father figure to your children. God is depending on you to show them how to trust in you so when they get a little older they'll automatically know how to trust in God, their spiritual father. Otherwise, what happens? They'll become like me, not fully trusting in God because there was no root of trust in God embedded inside me. There was no example of trusting in someone. So when I got old enough to understand God and his ways, I couldn't trust in him. It was extremely difficult. Just recently, while in prison, I began to learn how to depend on God wholeheartedly. I was tired of always being let down by people. No wonder none of my relationships had a chance to blossom–I didn't know how to trust! And where there's no trust, fear is there.

I simply made up my mind to believe that God loves me! I just kept telling myself, I trust God to do this or that. When I made that decision, God began to manifest or make himself real to me. Always keep in mind that a decision is an open door to reality. I experienced, and still am experiencing, the reality of God in every area of my life. Why? Because I made a decision to!

I had to stop feeling sorry for myself because I didn't have a caring father. I began to believe that God is my father. I had to say it over and over again until it was a fact in my heart. God is my father. God is my father. God is my father! If you say that long enough, it really will change you! It will take root in your spirit man.

Today I enjoy an awesome relationship with my father, God. I'm always talking with him about things and how to do things his way. Whenever I need something, I just trust that he can do it and he does it! My father is awesome and my trust in him is getting stronger by the second, the minute, the hour, the day, the week, the month, the year, and the decade to come.

Maybe you have felt, or are still feeling, the pain that I experienced of not having a father around. Yes, it hurts very much. But you can overcome that pain of rejection by not rejecting the fact that God is your father. Begin with determination by speaking to yourself and others if need be that God is your father. You have to know that God is truly your father to really experience the care that he has for his sons who believe and see him as father.

Your father has provided super powers. They are meant to allow you to demonstrate your son status to men who don't know who they really are in Christ.

Anyone who stands out, who conquers, who is courageous, who is bold, who is smart, who is determined to win and happens to always win seems to be eligible to wear the "hero" badge in the view of others. But the question I have for you is, "Who taught the hero his heroic actions?" For example, do you remember Mr. Miyagi, the karate teacher who taught the Karate Kid how to stand out, be courageous, bold, and determined to win in a smart way? Even though the Karate Kid lost a few matches and even suffered through bumps and bruises, like a loving father, Mr. Miyagi was always there to lift him up when he was down and to train him even harder to bring the very best out of him. Mr. Miyagi didn't just pat the Karate Kid's sore knee or kiss his hurting hand. He challenged him even when the Karate Kid wanted to quit! I'm almost certain that every hero wanted to quit at some point in their training, but the teachers, the coaches, the instructors, the mentors (which are all forms of a father) didn't allow that disaster to happen.

The ultimate hero, Jesus Christ, wanted to quit in the Garden of Gethsemane, but he didn't! Why? He had the strength of the father. Remember the son, Jesus Christ, and God are one. Also keep in mind that since Jesus is in your heart, that makes you a Son of God, and you and God are one. This is a perfect reason why quitting should not be an option. Look with me at John 3:21,

*But he who does the truth comes to the light, that his deeds may be clearly seen, that they have been done in God.*

When you realize who you are in Christ, put what you have discovered about yourself into practice. Then, and only then, your life will shine like a superhero. Everyone who witnesses your glow will know you have been taught and trained by God.

The force that moves superheroes into action is the force of love. God is love and love is God. God wants you to win in life. He never wants to see you lose. He loves and cares about you so much that he has equipped you with every power that is inside him.

But as I close this chapter, I want to talk about a huge problem in the lives of many men today, which is that men don't believe that God really does love them. When you don't believe God loves you then there's no faith in God, and when there's no faith in God, he isn't pleased. And if God isn't pleased, then there are no results. Hebrews 11:6 says,

*But without faith it is impossible to please him.*

So why do men think this way? Because of two reasons: (1) men as young boys didn't receive the love of an earthly father, and (2) mama took them to church just to hear a traditional preacher scream and yell at them by preaching that God is going to get you or throw you into hell. How can God throw you into hell if you have believed in his son, Jesus Christ? Romans 10:9 says,

*That if you confess with your mouth the Lord Jesus and believe in your heart that God has raised him from the dead, you'll be saved.*

Saved from what? The very pit of hell! Or what about the world's most famous scripture, found in John 3:16,

*For God so loved the world that he gave his only begotten son, That whosoever shall believe him shall not perish but have everlasting life.*

So if a man believes and accepts God's only begotten son, and God promises man everlasting life because he loves that man, why would God do something bad or send that man to hell for doing something wrong?! In fact, God can't send a man to hell or cause bad things to happen to him. A man goes to hell only by not believing in Jesus Christ and rejecting him to come and live in his everyday life. Bad things happen to a man because he makes bad choices.

Did you know that God is married to a man who turns his back on God! Wow! I'm about to prove to you how much God really, truly loves you.

Married is a strong word, in other words, it means covenant! God hates divorce! And if you are divorced, I didn't write that God hates you, he hates the act of divorce. So what happens to the man that dies in the world who backslid or turned his back on God? Will he make it into heaven? Yes! Yes! How? Number one, God loves that man and that man did receive Jesus as Lord and Savior. Number two, God is married or in covenant with that man—that's simply his love and his promise. Why would God send a man to hell when he just said in his word he is married to the backslider? It's the same way with the prodigal son! Why did the father receive him back into the family, give him a gold ring, throw him a big welcome back party, and give him some more money? Because he loved his son! Because of sin, men die early and go home to be with the Lord, men who have Jesus Christ in their life. While on earth, they didn't live the good life that was promised. God is forgiving but nature isn't so forgiving. But God can come in and demonstrate his love by bringing healing, if you believe he loves you enough to do so.

God's love for you is unconditional. You can't do anything so wrong that he just stops loving you. Get rid of the old way of traditional thinking and begin right now by saying repeatedly to yourself, "God is in love with me!" The Bible says you can have what you say! You should continue to say, "God is in love with me." But say these words of confession with consistency as well. "Since God loves me, I don't fear. Since God loves me, I always win. Since God loves me, he prospers me. Since God loves me, he protects me. Since God loves me, he shows up every time I call on him. Since God loves me, he sent his son to die for me and for my sin. Therefore, I'll go to heaven and see my father, God. Since God loves me, I am his personal superhero, conquering in every area of my life and full of his supernatural powers." When you say that consistently, that's what you'll become.

To the man who happens to be reading this book at this very moment, God loves you!!! When you don't give up knowing that God loves you, that's when victory is nearer than you think. You may have bills in your face screaming pay up or the lights go out. Your wife may be screaming, "I want a divorce!" Don't give in. There's a way to fix things. One ultimate way is that you just simply change! You just begin to show her God's love, the love that never fails. She'll change—God will see to it!

Because you are operating in faith, it does not matter at all how big are the tasks that you are facing. You just know, as you stand tall as the superhero, that you are the shadow of your father who is standing beside you. Your father who is love, who is God.  And God is love and he loves you unconditionally. This love is counting on you! This love is your very own father, "God."

# Chapter Ten

## Super Section One: If you think that way, you'll be that way

*As a man thinks in his heart, so is he. (Proverbs 23:4)*

Look with me at Isaiah 55:7-8,

*Let the wicked forsake his way, and the unrighteous man his thoughts; Let him return to the Lord, and he will have mercy on him; and to our God, for he will abundantly pardon. For my thoughts are not your thoughts, nor are your ways my ways, says the Lord.*

Life itself brings many challenges, trials, and tribulations. In fact, Jesus said we'd have them! Why? To build character in us, so that we can maintain with a trusting heart the different levels of success that God has for his man, which would be you. But here's another fact. Although Jesus said that we were going to have tribulations, he also commanded us to be of good cheer! Why? Because he has already overcome his tribulations, making us aware that we can have a cheerful attitude and overcome our tribulations.

However, for the majority of men today, they have it backward by using this sorry religious statement when a tribulation comes into their life. Most men say, "Well, you know our ways are not God's ways and his thoughts are not our thoughts." That isn't what Isaiah was trying to say in that verse of scripture. As you can see, the prophet Isaiah in verse seven was talking to the wicked, unrighteous, unsaved, or the person without a relationship with God. He was saying, "Listen, you need to change your way of thinking, because the way you are thinking isn't the way God thinks and the way you are acting isn't the way God would act."

Please understand, man of God, God's thoughts and his ways are found in his word! When a man of God makes a solid decision to get into the word of God and meditate on it and grow into acting it out, then and only then will that man have the thoughts of God and walk the ways of God.

The thoughts of God will change your thinking; the ways of God will change your thinking; and when you change the way you think, your whole life will change. So if you desire to change into the man that God would have you to be, get into his word and think how he thinks, act like he acts, so that you can experience the good life. When you do things the right way, you'll get the right results!

I'll never forget the times I had when I always seemed to think negative thoughts and think on negative ways. I used to think that I could never win in life, so I didn't. I used to think that I'd lose, so I did. I used think that I wasn't good enough, so I wasn't. I used to think that I was bad enough, so I was. When I walked around feeling sorry for myself and extremely depressed at times, it was always generated from the way that I was thinking. After hearing over and over again from my spiritual father, Creflo Dollar, that change only happens when I change the way I think, I finally realized why my life was in a gutter! It was because my mind was in the gutter! I had grossly offensive thoughts lodging within the arena of my mind. The word of God will absolutely tell you why you are not succeeding in this life. Look with me at Jeremiah 4:14,

*O Jerusalem, wash your heart from wickedness, that you may be saved! How long shall your iniquitous and grossly offensive thoughts lodge within?*

Well, I ask you in a challenging way, how long will you allow grossly offensive thoughts to pollute your mind and make your life stink? Are you standing in the telephone booth about to suffocate and die?

Bust out of the booth with the mind of a superhero ready to take action! That's what you really are in Christ. Commit your thought to God's thoughts. Commit your ways to the ways of God. Roll your cares on over to your father God, the one who wants to see you succeed. Look with me at Proverbs 16:3,

*Roll your works upon the Lord, commit and trust them wholly to him; he'll cause your thoughts to become agreeable to his will, and so shall your plans be established and succeed.*

Line your thoughts and ways up with the way God thinks and acts. Dedicate yourself to them. It won't be long before you'll be testifying to others saying, "Since I've been thinking like God I live like him, I act like him, I have wisdom like him, I am prosperous like him, I shine like him, and I win like him." You now can understand why Jesus could so confidently confess to the world, "I am" because he thought "I am" before he became "I am!"

The golden master key for success to explode in your life is what you think of yourself. If you are a negative man, negativity is in your heart. Isn't that interesting you can think negativity, failure, and defeat for so long that it gets into your heart and you become that. Change isn't change until you have changed. Think positively about yourself. You have read about powers and rights that are given to you by God Almighty throughout this book. Think on those things. Practice them, for in doing so those powers will get into your heart and move you to unlock the treasure to your destiny.

I want to write more on this subject of thinking, as it is very vital to me. At one point in my life I missed it and blew it! I had this golden master key, and still do, but at that time I didn't want to unlock the superhero that was sleeping within because of fear, so read on so that you learn not to fall into this devastating trap. The truth hurts–I was a loser, because I thought that way! It's true, believe me: you think this way, you'll be that way.

## Super Section Two: You are what you think

*This book of the law shall not depart from your mouth, but you shall meditate in it day and night, that you may observe to do according to all that is written in it. For then you'll make your way prosperous, and then you'll have good success. (Joshua 1:8)*

The golden master key has been given to me and I have given it to you. It is the key that will unlock the good life–the "prosperous" spiritual and physical way of living. And it will lock away the bondage life–the "poverty" spiritual and physical way of living. Now, I must admit to you that after spending a year with Dr. Creflo Dollar, I still didn't pay any attention to the golden key he was trying to give me. I was too busy trying to please him instead of applying what he had taught me of "the ways of God," pleasing God first! I had to find out that if I'd please God, then he'd be pleased. It finally registered inside me here in prison that the answer to life is the way you think! Again, I say that this is totally the golden master key supported by love, which exists in life.

You may say, okay, brother Brooks, I desire to possess all the powers of God that God has given me shown in this book. I want to be a changed man. I want to use my imagination and word power. I want to be the righteousness of God. I want to be a covenant man. I desire to be a man of faith. I desire to dominate on this earth. I truly want to be a man of prayer. I sure can use a change of character. I desire to be the superhero that God wants me to be. Desiring and wanting these powers from God are good, but not good enough until you start desiring and

179

wanting to change your thinking! You see, men of God, these powers are already inside you! They are asleep, waiting for your thinking to wake them up. How? It's by meditating on the word of God concerning the powers within you. Meditation on the word of God in all areas of your life will always breed good success, like Joshua 1:8 says. Meditation is to think on, think about, to roll over and over again in your mind, or to ponder on. When you meditate, you are "thinking." Men of God, this is exactly where we are missing it! Perhaps you have been meditating on the words of your mother, father, teacher, coach or someone else you look up to, words like: "You'll never make it! You'll never be anything. You can't do anything right." When you ponder and roll over those words repeatedly that's exactly what you'll become. Yes, it is true that "You are what you eat," which means if you eat a lot of junk food your body will feel like junk, slow to move with no energy. If you eat a lot of fruit and vegetables, you'll become energetic, vibrant, and strong. Well, here's another true phrase: "You are what you think." If you'll take the word of God and think on it that's what you'll become.

Let me give you an example according to the word of God in Psalm 8:6,

*You have made him to have dominion over the works of your hands; you have put all things under his feet.*

In Chapter Six, you read about this power from God. It's the power to dominate this earth. How can you change that? Think on, think about, roll over and over again (which is meditating on) the fact God has given you dominion here on the earth! Keep saying it over and over again throughout your day, "I have dominion, I have dominion, I have dominion." Then start thinking about the areas in your life where you need to dominate. Get in your mind that all things are under your feet. When you diligently, consistently think on this, then that's what you'll become because you are what you think!

This is how you can awaken all the powers that are inside you right now through meditating on the word of God, the word that says that you can dominate. Your meditation time that you spend by thinking on who you are in Christ will move you to act on what you're thinking, and the results will be what Joshua 1:8 says, "You shall have good success."

This principle truly works. Just think about it: whenever you think negatively, you receive negative results, and whenever you thought fearful things you were either moved to do what you feared might happen and it happened or it just simply can come to pass. From this point on, I want you to know that you hold the golden master key, which is "as a man thinks in his heart, so is he." In any situation, in any circumstance, whether it has to do with you or others you may know or not know, you are a superhero! Think that way in any endeavor that life will bring. Always, always keep in the forefront of your mind that you are what you think.

## Super Section Three: Seeing and thinking how God sees and thinks about you

*Where there is no vision, the people perish. (Proverbs 29:18)*

It is amazing to me how effective an old nursery story can be even in today's world of technology. Back when I was a small child I used to watch and hear about this little train that struggled to chug up a hill. He'd say to himself out loud, "I think I can. I think I can. I think I can." The little train had a vision to climb up the hill. He kept right on thinking that way and chugging on until he moved his way up the hill and into success! What was his success? It was making it to the very top of the hill.

Can you see how powerful this children's story can be? It's designed to train the mind of a child to think his way into victory. It's the same principle that teenagers and adults could use to be effective in life. But here's a question for you. What if this train never pictured himself making it to the top of the hill? You're right; he'd have never made it. His vision gave him the words and his words gave him the chugging power to get to the top of the hill.

As you see in Proverbs 29:18, people (men) will perish because of no vision for their lives. Man of God, after discovering who you truly are in this book, you now need to have a vision of how God sees you. Please get this vital fact. It's so very important that you begin to think and see how God thinks and see you.

- God thinks and sees you as a man of love, joy, peace, patience, kindness, goodness, faith, meekness, and temperance.
- God thinks and sees you as a man who believes in him and his word instead of in people and their negative words.
- God thinks and sees you as a man who uses his power of imagination and watches over his words by speaking faith-filled words.
- God thinks and sees you as a man who is in covenant with him. He knows that you'll do your part and he cannot wait to do his part.
- God thinks and sees you as a man who will take authority and

dominate in any arena of any problem that comes your way.

- God thinks and sees you as a man of faith, who can accomplish anything by using this powerful force that created the worlds.
- God thinks and sees you as a man of prayer, who knows how to go before God and get the answers and solutions to the worldly troubles that the enemy may bring. This man, which is you, knows how to create a solitary place so that he can use another unique ability that he has to hear from God.
- God thinks and sees you as a man who walks in love, a man who demonstrates the love of God to his loved ones *and* his enemies! This man, which is you, understands that this is the most powerful force on the planet. He knows that love will never ever fail him and since the love of God is in him, he could never fail in life.
- God thinks and sees you as a man who thinks and sees himself the way God thinks and sees him. He thinks and has a vision of winning every single day.

Whatever your vision may be in life, it should totally be supported, rooted and grounded in the powers that you have discovered about yourself. See yourself winning. See yourself rich and wealthy doing what God called you to do. See yourself with a positive image, the image of God in you.

Sit down; gather yourself together wherever you may be in life. You know who you are, and you are learning increasingly about yourself through the word of God. The vision that you have today is preparing right now to manifest itself tomorrow, whether positive or negative. So, think positive! This statement is scriptural. Look with me at Habakkuk 2:3,

*For the vision is yet for an appointed time, but at the end it shall speak, and not lie; though it tarry, wait for it; because it will surely come, it won't tarry.*

Any man that hooks his life up with God will receive a vision from God. The vision that you receive from God will always be meant to help other people. Before God sent his son to the earth, he gave him (Jesus) a vision to save the world, which is a huge gathering of people. Although Jesus had a vision, he still had to be patient (be consistently the same) in fulfilling that vision. We must do the same, for without patience (a characteristic of Christ) you could very well mess up the lives of others. There is a perfect season for the vision to come to pass that will yield perfect results. Jesus is the perfect example–why? Because of his patience mixed with faith, you're saved! And you know who you are in Christ.

If you are a single man, you have an opportunity to go all out for God. Carry that vision with conviction in your heart, knowing that there are people who are depending on you to bring them life. Many men have a vision; they say that they are going to do this and that but they never step out–why? Fear of the unknown, so this type of man does not know who he really is in Christ. Can you see why it is so important to know who you really are? No man can fulfill his true destiny without knowing who he really is in Christ.

Women are attracted to men with vision, so if you are looking for a wife, step into that vision God has given you at the right time. You'll see that you have already won her over because she perceives that you are going somewhere in life. I know that marriage is of God and can be the greatest union on earth, if operated in the right way. I'm not married and never have been married, but I do know that to be a fact–why? It's in the word of God. A woman who becomes your wife has been assigned to your life to help support your vision. So when looking for a wife always go for the woman who speaks words of encouragement, words of edification, words of inspiration with words that will bring out the superhero in you. This is a woman's gift, the words that she speaks. Generally, a man marries a woman, not because of beauty, but because of the words that flow out of her mouth into his heart. But don't get me wrong–beauty is very, very important to me! God will give you the woman of your dreams, a woman that is beautiful on the inside, which causes her to look very beautiful on the outside.

If you are married and your marriage is dead or shaky, that's your fault. Things can change very drastically if you'll become who you really are in Christ. On top of that, get a whole new vision for yourself, your family, your goals, and your dreams in life–period!

This book was written to give you a whole new purpose for your life. Take everything that you have learned about yourself in this book and apply it to your life. Your main goal after reading this book is to renew your mind about who you really are in Christ. In fact, that's how change comes–by the renewing of your mind. Once you have taken what you have discovered about yourself and mixed all of God's given powers with a yielded heart, that's when the superhero will arise in you, giving you the victory and making you a conqueror. God has need of you. Please, I am with you, so be the man God has called you to be. Demonstrate his love and power to a world of people who don't know who they really are in Christ. In a sense, you are like a spiritual buffet, a buffet of powers that exist inside you. Pick from that power buffet and put those powers to use, so that you can save a variety of people who are truly hurting in the world today.

Superheroes are winners. They have a mindset of being victorious. They may fall sometimes, but they always come back out on top. They have hearts full of love and never tolerate fear. This book is a book of discovering, a book for someone who desires to change.

CHANGE, MAN OF GOD. CHANGE AND NEVER FORGET: VICTORY

ONLY COMES WHEN YOU KNOW GOD LOVES YOU.

## *GO SUPERHERO GO.*

*Note: All scripture quotations are from the New King James Version or the Amplified Version of the Holy Bible.*

Dear Hero,

I'm about to be released, this tormenting season of my life is about to be over! This time it's real. This book is about to be over as well. I really put my heart into it so that it can enter into your heart and cause change in your life. I made it! Just 2 weeks left here in the chain gang. I finished this book. It was rough and hard but I did not let you down. You were my motivation to keep writing. It's a wonderful feeling when a man operates in the love of God. It's now the end of Nov, 2005 YEAH! I missed Thanksgiving, my moms home cooking and the enjoyment of being around family and friends. What did I eat on Thanksgiving here in prison? Do you really want to know? The usual peanut butter and jelly and a boloney sandwich. That's ok. Though, I will be home for Christmas. Hey man of god, don't you ever quit! O.K I know you have probably discovered who you really are and it made seem like a lot, but that's what you are a lot of Gods power within you. Don't forget to apply what you know. If I can come out of prison alive and well as well as the accomplishment of this book. Surely you can come out of the box (like the telephone booth) of life. And declare to the world the superhero that you have discovered to be. YOU ARE GOD'S MAN. But before I end this book with you, there is something that I do not want you to ever forget and those are my final words to you which will be found on the next page. My blessings are forever with you.

BROOKS

187

## The Man who thinks he can

If you think you are beaten, you are
If you think you dare not, you don't
If you would like to win but you think you can't
It's almost a cinch you won't

If you think you'll lose, you've lost
For out in the world we find,
Success begins with a fellow's will,
It's all in the state of mind

If you think you're outclassed, you are
You've got to be sure of yourself
Before you can ever win a prize.

Think big and your deeds will grow
Think small and you'll fall behind
Think that you can, and you will
It's all a state of mind.

Life's battles don't always go to the
Stronger or the faster man,
But sooner or later, the man who wins
Is the man who thinks he can.

**Though he stumble, he will not fall,
for the LORD upholds him with his hand.**

**Psalm 37:24 NIV**

Cover art and all illustrations
designed by
**DIVINE IMAGE GRAPHICS**
Atlanta, GA
info@divineimagegraphics.com